BUSINESS

etiquette

MADE EASY

BUSINESS

etiquette

MADE EASY

The Essential Guide to Professional Success

Myka Meier

FOUNDER OF
THE PLAZA HOTEL'S FINISHING PROGRAM

Skyhorse Publishing

Skyhorse Publishing books may be purchased in bulk at special discounts for sales promotion, corporate gifts, fund-raising, or educational purposes. Special editions can also be created to specifications. For details, contact the Special Sales Department, Skyhorse Publishing, 307 West 36th Street, 11th Floor, New York, NY 10018 or info@skyhorsepublishing.com.

Skyhorse® and Skyhorse Publishing® are registered trademarks of Skyhorse Publishing, Inc.®, a Delaware corporation.

Visit our website at www.skyhorsepublishing.com.

10 9 8 7 6 5 4

Library of Congress Cataloging-in-Publication Data is available on file.

Cover design by Daniel Brount

Print ISBN: 978-1-5107-5193-4
Ebook ISBN: 978-1-5107-5196-5

Printed in China

To my entrepreneur father Adrian, who encouraged me as a young girl to start my first business, always telling me "be your own boss." To my mother Bonnie, a female CEO for over twenty-five years, who is my constant sounding board and loving guide, and to my amazing, supportive husband Marco, who first encouraged me to open Beaumont Etiquette and to never, ever, ever give up—thank you!

To my business partner Anne Chertoff, who contributed to this book with her great wit and wisdom. Thank you for always being by my side, making every day fun, and being brave enough to always say yes to seemingly impossible feats.

Contents

Introduction

What if I told you I knew some of the most successful businesspeople in the world and they all shared one major secret to success, no matter their industry—would you want to know what it was? Now, imagine that you too could learn this secret, and some of the same techniques that these successful businesspeople practice from day to day. I bet you'd really be interested in that, right? It differentiates them from everyone else, and has given these people the upper hand in both their professional and personal lives. Anyone can learn it, and once you have this knowledge, you can use it every single day to get ahead.

The big secret? Believe it or not, these people understand, value, and practice good etiquette. You see, etiquette is not commonly taught in most schools anymore. Not even in many of the Ivy League institutions. So, in addition to your textbook education, those who have an education in etiquette stand out in major ways because they have gone above and beyond traditional schooling to achieve a higher level of skill and learning. I like to call it the "next level" of education, especially in business. These people are therefore the best in exercising it because they sought after this skill set in addition to the traditional means of learning. They took it upon themselves to absorb and practice it, and because they choose to do so, they can recognize and appreciate others in business who have done the same. Sometimes you may be forced to go to school, but nobody is forced to practice good etiquette. It's a choice.

So, how do I know this secret is the common denominator for so many successful professionals? It's because I've had the great privilege to work with and advise human resources team members, training and development offices, recruiting departments, and internal leadership teams of some of the largest and most profitable companies in the world. My team and I have gotten an inside look at what sets a candidate apart, what makes a company invest in a person, and what makes an employee excel. We have sat with leading CEOs and heard what is important to them and their companies, and have traveled the country training and consulting businesses in all industries and levels, from start-ups to Fortune 100 companies. All would likely agree that while there are some major recurring themes to a successful professional, one umbrella theme that spans across almost all of them is that of business etiquette.

Now, it could be that you are just starting your career, are currently interviewing for your dream job, transitioning to another industry, already on your way up the ladder, or just want to revamp your professional image. Regardless of what level you are at, the good news is that you're already one step ahead of everyone else, because you recognize the importance of including etiquette in your everyday professional life. The even better news is that you're in the right place! Throughout this book, you'll learn techniques and tips that will catapult you to the next level of your career time and time again. Through easy-to-follow chapters, I'll teach you tried-and-tested methods that you can start using today to instantly set you apart. Ready to get started?

Did You Know?

Where does the word "etiquette" come from anyway? According to Merriam-Webster, one definition of the French word *étiquette* is "ticket" or "label attached to something for identification." In sixteenth-century Spain, the French word was borrowed (and altered to "*etiqueta*") to refer to the written protocols describing orders of precedence and behavior demanded of those who appeared in court. Eventually, "*etiqueta*" came to be applied to the court ceremonies themselves as well as the documents that outlined the requirements for them. Interestingly, this then led to French speakers of the time attributing the second sense of "proper behavior" to their "*étiquette*," and, in the middle of the eighteenth century, English speakers finally adopted both the word and the second meaning from the French.

Chapter 1

Polished Professional

Etiquette and Why It Matters

Whether you're convinced or not yet that an education in etiquette is one of the skills that sets successful professionals apart from all the rest, this next bit may put you over the edge of being a believer. This statistic is so powerful that I even keep it on both my general website (beaumontetiquette.com) and my corporate training website (beaumonttraininggroup.com).

A Harvard-Stanford study concluded that one's success, particularly in the workplace, is based 85 percent on social skills, and less than 15 percent on technical skill set.

Now, let's think about that. This essentially means you could be the smartest person in the room, with the highest IQ on the team, but if your emotional intelligence or EQ (emotional quotient) is not high, then you still have a lot of area for improvement. In fact, I would rather have a higher EQ than IQ any day. Emotional intelligence is crucial in connecting with people, responding to people, and generally being likable. Your emotional intelligence determines your understanding and awareness of and compassion toward others when communicating both verbally and nonverbally. From the moment people with high emotional intelligence walk into a room, they know how to act, carry themselves, and respond in order to make others feel comfortable. Ultimately, everyone wants to work with these people. They are social chameleons in the way that they can adjust and readjust as needed.

This sounds like a pretty great quality to have in business, right? Whether it be speaking to your boss, presenting to potential new clients, entering an interview, networking at a big event, or hosting a dinner, people who can walk into a room and feel at ease no matter what, are incredibly valuable and a great asset to have on any team. So, can EQ be learned? Absolutely! You don't have to be born with it, and you can learn techniques to help you increase your emotional intelligence, especially when it comes to business.

I start every training by explaining what everyday etiquette actually means. So, what does etiquette *really* mean in practical terms? There is a common misconception that etiquette is only used when we are in nice or "fancy" places. This couldn't be further from the truth. Etiquette should be used every day and everywhere you go, and especially in business. The core of what good etiquette in business means is to be kind, respectful, and considerate to all around you. From how you interact in an office environment and the way you treat your colleagues, to the way you present yourself, etiquette is the protocol we follow to show respect to others.

No matter if you're in a meeting or interview or at a business lunch, there are countless examples of how having bad etiquette can break a business deal. A partner of a very successful company once told me his secret hiring process: when it came down to the top two or three candidates, he would take them all out to lunch individually. While the candidate was so focused on answering his technical questions over the meal, he was actually observing and paying special attention to their social and dining manners throughout the meal. From the way they spoke to the server to the way they ate their lunch and everything in between, he told me he wanted to see what his clients would see when they were being entertained or brought to lunch to talk business. His favorite part was seeing if they were respectful to the service personnel working at the restaurant, from the hostess and server to the coat-check person, because his belief was that if they were disrespectful or dismissive to those helping, then surely that's how they would treat their future team members.

How to Make a Great First Impression

There is a lot of pressure around making the best first impression. When thinking about this, we immediately tend to think about what we wear and how we comb our hair, but did you know that in many cases, your first impression is not in person? A first impression can be your voice through a phone call, an email, or even your social media content. According to a 2018 Career Builder Survey, 70 percent of employers use social media to screen candidates during the hiring process, and about 43 percent of employers use social media to check on current employees. The even more startling part is that what comes up when they search online for you matters. Of the companies that do social media research, 57 percent have found content that caused them not to hire candidates. When a company searches for you online, it's important to note that what usually pops up first are the sites we are on that have the highest search engine optimization (SEO), so think about all your social media channels.

Tip Time!

When's the last time you Googled yourself? If it's more than three months ago, make it your homework to do a general as well as Google Image search for your name so you know what other people see when they look you up online! Master tip: Set a Google alert for your name so you always know when you are mentioned online.

What Makes a Great In-Person First Impression?

Let's think about why it's important for us to make a positive first impression, specifically in business. We want people to like us, work with us, hire us, respect us, and invest in us. The root of business is professionalism and respect, and people have to buy into that as soon as they meet us. Plain and simple, trust is built on first impressions. As an example, let's use the below photos to show an extreme case: how a first impression can make or break perceived professionalism.

Look at the images above. If you were walking into your doctor's office and the woman on the left greeted you, you'd likely be pretty happy trusting her with your health care. Now let's look at the woman on the right. If this woman walked in to examine you, you'd probably jump off the exam table and ask to see her ID proving credentials, right? In fact, the person in the right-hand image is the same person shown on the left, only she is presented differently. From her posture to her clothing and grooming routine, you made a judgment. Case in point, this shows how no matter the industry, a first impression is what makes (or breaks) the trust of others in business.

Now, let's talk about how long you have to make your first impression, and how you can always ensure you're making a great one. First impressions are made up of a few different components, where one without the next renders the whole first impression. Have you ever heard that you have seven seconds to make a first impression? There are different variations of this theory, with some people saying within milliseconds the other person you interact with already has made an opinion about you.

What's the Meier Method?
In my first book, *Modern Etiquette Made Easy*, I introduced the Meier Method, a five-step process to becoming instantly more polished and confident through etiquette!

I created the "7-in-7 Theory," because of the seven successful elements I consistently see after years of observing incredible first impressions. The number seven recurs in this section, because many people believe you have seven seconds to make a first impression. The seven aspects to a great in-person first impression are:

1. Physical Placement
The way you physically enter a room can show confidence and authority, or a lack thereof. It can also show that you are friendly and approachable, or quite the contrary. It's up to you how you want to be perceived. On page 15 I'll teach you the one thing you should always do when entering a room.

2. Facial Control
According to psychologists Janine Willis and Alexander Todorov in their *Psychological Science* article "First Impressions," it takes only a tenth of a second to make a judgment on the face alone. For this

reason, you must be hyperaware that even the slightest positive change in your expression can say you are approachable, friendly, and ready to do business.

3. Personal Presentation

Always dress the way you want to be addressed. The way you want to be perceived is up to you! Do you want to come across as a corporate professional or a creative director? Either one is absolutely fantastic depending on your personal and professional goals. Your clothing and grooming are representative of your professional self. More on style and grooming to come (page 26).

4. Posture

When is the last time you saw a powerful professional hunched over a boardroom table while speaking to their team or slouching while giving a presentation to a huge audience? Posture is the one point of body language that can instantly change the way people perceive you. You can go from confident and self-assured to insecure and lacking authority within a single second by showing poor posture. More on posture to come (page 37).

5. Voice

Your voice is a tool to tell people how confident, assertive, and powerful of a presence you have. You would never see a major CEO of a huge firm speaking softly when addressing his or her team, and you certainly wouldn't see a successful salesperson pitching a potential client with a high squeaky voice or a low one that trails off at the end of each sentence. You could be the best and most powerfully dressed person in the room, but if you open your mouth and it doesn't match your appearance, you are doing yourself a major disservice. More about your voice in chapter 2 (page 43).

6. Body Language (Including Eye Contact)

The way you carry yourself is crucial. Are you ready to take on the day or are you tired and bored and not wanting to be there? Your body can tell everyone in the room how you are feeling without you saying a single word. Try out some of our body language secrets in chapter 5 (page 79) to win in every situation.

7. Charisma

Charisma is a characteristic held by people of great persuasion and influence. Charisma is charm, or evoking positive emotion in someone else, and it can be learned. It's what draws others toward you, and it stems from your attitude and emotional state. People who make others feel good, empowered, and happy through a winning combination of body language, words, and actions are often seen as charismatic in business.

The overarching theme to the 7-in-7 theory, particularly in business, is professionalism. Being professional shows that you are serious about your career and is also one of the most important attributes of a great leader. Both companies and clients value professionalism, which is key to a successful working relationship. Look at the list below of attributes and qualities, and ask yourself on how many your HR team or boss would score you a ten out of ten? On how many would you score yourself a ten out of ten? Ideal candidates at most companies will rate a seven or higher in every category. The great news is that all of these attributes are skills you can improve upon.

Professionalism

Image and Appearance: Do you look the part both in the way you dress and groom yourself?

Organization and Preparation: From your appearance and presentation materials to your to-do list, are you clear, focused, and efficient?

Competence: Are you capable of your skill and ability, needing little hand-holding?

Knowledge and Expertise: Do you know your industry, craft, and service inside and out at the level you are at?

Accountability: Are you responsible?

Honesty and Integrity: Are you honest, truthful, and trustworthy?

Practicing Good Etiquette: Are you respectful, kind, and considerate?

Reliability: Can your coworkers count on you no matter what? The most valuable player in many instances is the first one in and the last one to leave.

Maintaining Poise at All Times: In high-pressure situations, can you keep your cool?

Work Ethic: Do you work incredibly hard and are proactive in your actions, always taking initiative and doing the best you can?

Demeanor: Are you personable, likable, and friendly?

Greetings

To help when you are meeting and greeting people, I created the Meier Method's HACH (**H**andshake, **A**ir kiss, **C**heek kiss, **H**ug) System of Greeting. These are the four most formal ways to greet people in the Western world.

The Handshake

The handshake in business is always appropriate. It's the most professional greeting and a good one shows confidence and trust. The only time I would give any other greeting is if my client or superior who is greeting me initiated something different. When in doubt for social or business greetings, always go for the handshake.

Bonus Personal Presentation

Personal presentation does not just mean what you wear and how you are groomed. It also includes what you are carrying! Whether it be a lunch meeting with a client, a catch-up with your boss, or an interview, you should pay just as close attention to what is in your hands as you do everything else. For instance, you might look super sharp in a tailored suit or nice outfit, but the moment you pull out your old spiral notebook with paper flying out of the sides or your chewed pen, you don't look nearly as polished as you could. Often things like cell phone covers, briefcases, and items we carry with us every day tend to look shabby instead of business-chic, but we tend not to notice because we see them every day. Someone seeing them for the first time, though, may certainly notice. Check the quality ahead of time for items such as your notebook, pen, briefcase or whatever bag you carry into a meeting, presentation folder, cell phone case, business card holder, wallet, and cases of any electronics you carry with you like an iPad or computer.

Your handshake is your physical signature. Always remember that. What does it say about you and the way you do business? Years ago, I was working with a team tasked with hiring positions at all levels for a new department. We were holding group interviews due to the massive number of applicants, and in this case, their first impressions were crucial. Each group only had ten minutes to interview in a roundtable-style format before the hiring team reconvened to choose who would move forward to one-on-one interviews.

Each candidate in the room was technically qualified and had the education and experience we were looking for; however, it was a client-facing job in financial sales that needed team members with a strong presence. Instead of taking the time to weed candidates out on the phone, they were invited into this rather challenging group interview environment to see who stood out.

As each roundtable ensued, it became clear who would move on almost immediately due in part to that initial first impression, which comes largely from a handshake. So many people had weak handshakes that we instantly didn't feel they were confident or self-assured enough to be on the team. It came down to eight candidates we really thought were strong enough to move to the next level, with one other wavering. Half of the hiring team thought the wavering man may be a great fit, while the other half thought he may be too shy for an outward sales role. In the end, the HR director had the tie-breaking vote. She voted yes for him to come through as the ninth interviewee, and can you guess why? She said while although he didn't verbalize as loudly as some of the other candidates, she instantly felt "safe" in the way he greeted her. His handshake was firm, his smile gentle and trusting, and his eye contact unwavering. The end of the story is even better, as he was one of the three candidates hired in the end and turned out to be a star team member, constantly ranking in the top of his level, no doubt because he had the ability to make everyone he greeted know they were in good hands (pun intended).

Did You Know?

The history of the handshake dates back to the fifth century B.C. in Greece and was used as a symbol of peace. The hand-to-hand gesture was used by two people to prove to one another that both parties had no weapons.

Rules of the Handshake

1. Always extend your right hand so that you shake the other person's right hand. Open your hand angled at about 30 degrees so that the web of your hand meets the web of the other person's hand.

2. Always stand to shake a hand. To shake hands while seated in any business environment, whether at a boardroom table or a dining table, shows laziness and can be seen as a lack of respect to the person whose hand you are shaking.

3. No matter the gender of the person's hand you are shaking, you should squeeze their hand in a firm and assertive, yet never aggressive, way. The most common issue I see with handshakes is that they are not firm enough. A soft handshake shows lack of confidence. Practice your handshake at home with a friend or trusted colleague and ask them to give you constructive criticism. Be ready to hear the honest truth, because you'd rather know earlier so you can improve it, rather than later in a business situation that causes your first impression to be a weak one due to your handshake.

4. Unless you are trying to assert authority over another person when shaking hands, I advise you never to put one hand on top of the other person's hand. I often hear people say they think this is a sign of warmth, but this is actually a sign of power. Some of my clients who are going into business negotiations use this as a "power play" tactic. Please just never do this to your boss!

5. In business, we shake hands using two pumps of the hand, and in social situations, we use three pumps. This is because in business we get straight to the point, but socially we often have a little bit more to talk about, and need that extra pump. If the person whose hand you are shaking doesn't let go, just go with it so you don't offend them by pulling away.

6. Make eye contact. The entire time you are shaking hands, and even after the handshake is over, continue to lock eyes with the person you are greeting. Have you shaken someone's hand and as you are doing so, they are looking over your shoulder at someone else in the room? Not only does it feel awful to be on the receiving end of that in terms of not feeling important, but it also makes the entire handshake feel disingenuous. Even after however many pumps of the hand, if you are still talking, eye contact should still be made.

The Air Kiss

The air kiss is what we do socially. It is when we lean in and we put our right cheek to the other person's right cheek. We do touch cheeks, but very gently, and our actual lips never touch the skin of the other person's cheek. When you lean in, take your right hand and gently place it on the other person's right elbow or the outside of their forearm. This also helps you determine if someone is coming in for a second kiss. You don't need to make any kissing noises when you do so. It is also important to remember that we always follow the etiquette and customs of the country and culture we are in. This means you must know how many kisses are appropriate in each country, as it can vary slightly. For example, in the United States we offer one kiss, right cheek to right cheek. In the United Kingdom, we offer two kisses, starting first with one kiss on the right cheek, then one kiss on the left cheek. In other countries in Europe, such as Switzerland for example, we offer three kisses. One kiss on the right cheek, one on the left, and a third on the right cheek again.

The Cheek Kiss

This is reserved for close friends, family, and children in private. The cheek kiss is often incorrectly practiced in public at social events, often ending with a person walking around a cocktail party with a lipstick stain on their cheek, which shouldn't happen. The cheek kiss is when the lips actually touch the cheek of the person we are kissing. All other rules of the air kiss still apply otherwise.

The Hug

Very similar to the cheek kiss, the hug is also only reserved for close friends, family, and children in private.

Introductions

When introducing people, there are three "orders of introduction" that should be followed to show respect. If someone knows these rules, they might be offended if introduced incorrectly. So, who is introduced first? When you are trying to decide who to introduce first, think to yourself, *who do I want to show respect to first?* The three orders of introductions are as follows, and are listed by order of importance:

1. **The most important person** ("President Collingwood, may I please introduce you to Mr. Volney.")

2. **The most senior in age** ("Grandpa, may I please introduce you to my colleague Anne?")

3. **Gender** (If everyone in the room is the same level of rank, you would say the female names first, followed by the male names.)

If all of the above are standing in the same room, simply say the name of the person who you want to honor first, and rarely will you ever go wrong. If you are introducing one person to a group of people and you don't know all their names or it would just take ages to introduce them all, start with the highest-ranking person first and then let everyone else introduce themselves. For example, "Doctor Pullman, may I please introduce you to the new team of residents starting here at the hospital this fall?" Each person would then step forward and introduce themselves.

If your boss and their partner are at an event and you are in charge of introducing them, remember that a married couple take on the same status. So, if you are introducing your boss Adrian, and he is standing with his wife Diane, you would say "Adrian and Diane, may I please introduce you to our new associate Charles?"

"May I please" is the correct formal way to introduce people. Don't "mirror introduce" which means "Bonnie, please meet Peter. Peter, this is Bonnie," which is what I often hear. It gives them nothing to talk about and no detail to start a conversation. A good introduction would give a small bit of information about each person so that they can carry on conversation without you. For example, "Bonnie, may I please introduce you to our new Advertising Associate Peter, who just moved here from New Jersey. Bonnie has been the director of our sales division for the past two years and oversees all our teams."

Addressing People

Here are the most common titles, what they mean, and when to use them:

- **Mrs.**—Used when addressing a married woman
- **Miss**—Used when addressing an unmarried young woman under the age of eighteen

Making an Entrance

As the first step in the 7-in-7 theory is physical placement, whether it's a boardroom you are entering or a single office for an interview, try this tip next time you make an entrance. When you walk through a door, never turn your back to those already in the room. This means while you walk through the door-way, close the door with your left hand so that your right hand stays open to meet, greet, and shake hands. By not turn-ing your back to those in the room you are entering, your body language is sharp and you make eye contact instantly, which in business is a trustworthy gesture.

- **Ms.**—Used when addressing a woman over the age of eighteen or if you are unsure if she is married
- **Mr.**—Used when addressing a man
- **Mstr.**—Short for Master, and used when addressing a young man under the age of eighteen
- **Mx.**—Used when addressing a person who doesn't want to be identified by gender; pronounced miks

- **Dr.**—Used when addressing someone who has earned either a medical doctorate (MD) or a doctorate in academics (PhD)

How to Exude Confidence, Authority, and Charisma

Have you ever wondered why some people excel more than others in business? These people don't seem to have more advantages than anyone else, yet they always succeed in whatever they do? If you divide out what it is that makes someone engaging, it's a combination of confidence, authority, and charisma. I witnessed a perfect example of these attributes recently when watching two different people present their ideas to a global marketing and public relations company. The company was hiring a new team member and was stuck between two candidates, so for the final deciding factor, the potential hires were asked to deliver a mock presentation. I was asked to sit in on the presentations to help give feedback.

As we all sat back to observe, both candidates walked up to the small podium area giving a great first impression. Both were impeccably dressed, groomed, and experienced. They each had ten minutes to present and five minutes to answer questions. Each person took out their laptops and set up their presentations and were equally as organized. Both presentations were incredibly thoughtful, but Candidate B's presentation was significantly more strategic than Candidate A's. In fact, had we just been reading through the two presentations, we all would have unanimously voted on Candidate B to get the job. At the end of the presentations however, Candidate A got every single last vote of the judging committee. So, why did Candidate A get the job in the end?

While both started off strong in appearance, Candidate A started off with a joke that made a tense room smile. The presentation was delivered with such power, purpose, and authority, that we all felt like we wanted to sign up for whatever this person was selling.

Candidate B was a bit softer spoken, serious, and nervous. We all agreed that we actually enjoyed the first presentation so much that we didn't want it to end! Everyone wanted this person on their team. Candidate A was offered the job with a high-paying salary, a great team, and stellar clients.

About a month later, I checked in with the company to see how the onboarding process was going with Candidate A. They told me that unfortunately when they offered Candidate A the job, the person had four competing offers already on the table and went with another company! Disappointed to hear this, I asked if they had therefore started onboarding Candidate B into the new role. The HR director told me that after they saw Candidate A's presentation skills, they couldn't see anyone with less of a presence in the role and decided to extend the search time to find another person with a similar *wow* factor, who had equal confidence and presence.

This story is a perfect example of how someone who exudes confidence and authority wins in business time and time again. Sometimes it matters less about what you're saying and more about *how* you say it. There is an old saying that when someone is convincing through words and personality "they could sell ice to an Eskimo." I often say this to myself when I come across someone like Candidate A. In business, "confidence is king." Why? Confidence is what we project and what we want others to see. Confidence can change momentarily, but is what we want to see from a business person. Self-esteem is something that often takes months or even years to build, while confidence can be learned, emulated, controlled, and portrayed situationally with just a few tips.

> ### Pens and Ink: What's Appropriate?
> The most formal ink color in business is black, followed by blue. The exterior of the pen in business should be either a dark color such as black, navy blue, or maroon, or a metallic color such as gold or silver. A company pen with the logo branded on it is also perfectly appropriate to use.

The Meier Method Formula for Confidence

1. **Package yourself.** From your appearance to your pen, package yourself in a polished manner.

2. **Use your voice.** Your voice should be powerful (this is different than loud!) and controlled.

3. **Build rapport.** Build close relationships with people you do business with so that you feel comfortable with them and vice versa.

4. **Understand what "sparks" you.** Make a list of things that you'd like to feel more confident in, then challenge yourself to work on each point.

5. **Organize yourself.** Being organized helps you think clearly and be more efficient.

6. **Emulate others.** Watch others whose confidence you admire, and channel that energy.

7. **Practice!** Practice your new confident self all the time. Call it your confident alter ego if you'd like, but you need to learn how to

turn it on and off in business, and if you only use it when you are presented with a situation you are not confident in, it won't work. Don't fake it until you make it, practice it until you become it!

The Meier Method Formula for Authority

1. Use your voice. Remember, a strong voice will command attention

2. Express powerful body language. Showing you are powerful through your posture and stance tells people you are in charge without hearing a single word out of your mouth.

3. Talk more, but only when relevant. Use facts, statistics, or stories when speaking to make your point.

4. Make decisions. Be confident in a choice or decision and express it. Instead of saying "I agree," say "I think we should do _____."

5. Be confident. See the Meier Method for Confidence above!

6. Get rid of fear. If you don't do something, say something, apply for something, etc., because you are fearful, you are the only person preventing yourself from achieving your goals.

The Meier Method Formula for Charisma

If you can remember this, then you are already one step ahead: Charm is simply a state of mind, with the goal to evoke positive emotion in someone else. That's it! Easy, right? Every time you are talking to someone new in a business situation such as a networking event, simply try to evoke positive feelings in the other person. It could be through humor, a compliment, asking a great question to show genuine interest, or even a nice gesture. Charm is your secret weapon in the workplace. The components to remember are as follows:

1. Maintain a positive attitude. No matter how bad a morning you've had, always walk in without complaining and a smile on your face. Nobody wants to work with a negative person.

2. Create the best first impression. Follow the steps of the 7-in-7 theory on page 5.

3. Create a likable persona. Do people want to spend time with you? Three of the most likable characteristics are friendliness, sincerity, and happiness.

4. Project confidence. See the Meier Method for Confidence on page 18!

5. Change negative perceptions. Change negative perceptions people may have about you such as "he always shows up late for meetings" or "she never speaks up on conference calls."

6. Overcome fear. You can do it!

7. Surround yourself with happy people. Happy people are the most attractive. Build rapport, spend time asking people genuine questions, and the next time you see those people, bring up the last conversation you had to show you were paying attention and that you care!

8. Stand out . . . humbly! It's okay to think differently. As Oscar Wilde's once said, "Be yourself. Everyone else is taken." You don't want to be a wallflower, but nobody likes a colleague who brags either. Sometimes it matters less about what you're saying and more about *how* you say it.

How to Take Credit without Bragging

Whether you are in an interview or have just given a presentation, it's important to always be humble about yourself and your success. For example, I often give keynote speeches across America on a number of different topics. The last time I gave one, the president of the company told me how much his team loved my presentation. While I said thank you and accepted the compliment, I was also careful to remain modest by saying "I truly couldn't have done it without my amazing team!" Modesty is a great quality to have for anyone in a position of success.

You may notice a good amount of repeat in the above three formulas, but if you look closely, you'll see that the order in which each point shows up in order of importance from top to bottom vastly changes, depending on the effect we want to have on others.

Words and Phrases to Remove from Your Vocabulary

- "Sorry"—Many people say the word "sorry" way too much in business, often misusing it.
- "Can I ask a quick question?"—Asking permission in business makes you submissive. Stop doing it, and instead simply say what you want. For example, "I'd like to add in _____."

- "Just"—This word should be taken out of your business vocabulary. For example, "I just need a minute," implies that you are begging for a quick moment of someone's time and that you are not worthy of more than that! Worse are phrases like, "I was just hoping you would consider . . ." or "it's just a simple task." Using the word "just" in this context takes away any sort of importance behind your question or statement.

- "Pardon me"—Unless you are in the service staff industry, you don't need to ask for a pardon. Instead, a "please excuse me" will do.

- "I can't"—When your boss asks you to complete a task and you don't have the time or capacity to take on more work, it's easy to tell your boss that you can't do it. I can assure you, however, that this is not what your boss wants to hear. Instead, try to say you'd be happy to tackle more work with some extra resources/time/whatever it is you will need to accomplish the task. You can also say you are currently working on XYZ and ask your boss how they would like you to prioritize your tasks, and proceed in that order.

- "To be honest with you . . ."—This phrase implies that maybe you haven't been honest in the past. Avoid phrases that may give someone a reason to doubt your trustworthiness.

Can you think of a business scenario in which you need to use confidence, authority, and charisma? One example is making a toast or speech! Years ago, when I was living in London, my boss and a few of my junior colleagues and I hosted a big group of clients from New York out to a nice dinner. Halfway through the dinner, one of the clients mentioned to my boss that it was her colleague's birthday that day, the senior director of the company. Because my boss wasn't feeling well that day, he asked me to give a toast. Upon hearing this,

I instantly froze in terror. I had never given a toast to three tables of people before, but I was the second most senior person from my company, so it was my job to take over. I remember running to the bathroom with my phone to Google "how to give a toast" and feeling dizzy scrolling through endless blogs and websites with tips. I don't even quite remember what ended up coming out of my mouth, but I fear it was embarrassingly amateur and I'd like to forget it! Had I known then what I know now, I wouldn't have needed to panic! To this day, in both my personal and professional life, I still use the technique that follows.

Giving Toasts and Speeches

First, let's talk about the difference between a toast and a speech. A toast is a short (sometimes impromptu) congratulatory address to an audience to recognize a person, group of people, or an occasion. A speech is a much longer formal address to an audience that is often written and rehearsed at great length. The best speeches I have ever seen are so rehearsed that the speaker knows it by heart and doesn't have to read from cue cards or a monitor. If you are asked to give a speech, you will likely be given a good deal of notice, because both the writing and practice of a speech can be time-consuming.

To always give a strong toast, all you need do is follow a technique called Past-Present-Future, and remember to keep it short! When you need to give a toast, simply say something either about the person, company, or people you are toasting to that previously happened, then you say something from today, and then you say something about what is yet to come. Let me give you an example below:

Scenario: You are asked to give a toast to your client XYZ Consulting Group at a holiday dinner to thank them for another amazing year.

Toast: Good evening everyone, and thank you for coming to our annual holiday dinner. I'd like to take a moment and raise a glass to thank the incredible team at XYZ Consulting Group for three years of dedicated service (*past*). We are so delighted you could be here with us today to celebrate a wonderful and successful year, thanks to you, our valuable partners (*present*). I, along with my team, look forward to many more successful years to come (*future*), and bravo for your amazing work this year. To XYZ—cheers!"

The above format works in every situation I can think of. A few more common questions I hear are answered below:

Q: When should you stand?

A: If you are giving a toast at a small table and everyone can hear you easily, there is no need to stand. If, however, you are giving a toast to multiple tables in a room, you should stand so your voice projects to everyone at each table.

Q: When does a toast or speech take place?

A: A toast typically serves as a welcome. It is customary to toast at the very beginning of the evening after everyone has arrived and had time to get settled with a drink and hors d'oeuvres.

Q: Who should give a toast or speech?

A: The host of the event or one of the most senior representatives of a company in attendance.

Q: Should the audience reply with a clap or something verbal?

A: If one person is at the reciprocating end of a toast, perhaps for a birthday, then the person who was just honored may choose to give a thank-you toast back. They would follow the same guidelines of the person who gave the toast. So, if someone just gave me a birthday toast, I might reciprocate with "Thank you for such a lovely toast! I have loved being a part of the team for the past five years, I'm so lucky to be here tonight celebrating with you all, and wishing many more celebrations with you all to come!" If the person giving the toast ends it with "To David" and raises their wine or champagne glass at the same time they say David's name, the audience would raise their glasses in turn and repeat back "To David!"

Q: How do I get everyone's attention to give the toast?

A: I verbally and very loudly (or get someone who has a booming voicc to help you) say "Excuse me, everyone!" until everyone looks up, which can be done on a microphone for larger groups. If all else fails, the typical "clinking" of a glass with a piece of silverware against a glass typically works, as people tend to chime in and clink their own glasses until everyone is silent. The issue with this and why I don't like to use it unless nothing else has worked, is because while you are hitting the silverware against the glass to make noise, you also risk cracking a glass.

You Are a Brand

Just like we think of our favorite products as part of a brand, you are also a brand. When you join a company, you take on a part of the brand's identity and are expected to maintain it. You serve as an extension of the brand at all times, whether it be on your social media accounts, in a client meeting, or even at a bar after work. I tell my clients to start thinking of themselves as a two-pronged brand. You are your own walking, talking, breathing billboard, with your own style and personality that you present to others. At the same time, your brand falls under the umbrella of your company's brand. People who are "on brand" for a company are much more likely to get hired and promoted. Being on brand is not purely a function of how you present yourself but also of how you interact and communicate with your colleagues and clients. It is about having a positive attitude about the company, your projects, and your team.

Now, this doesn't mean you have to fit some exact mold or robotic nature of a "perfect" company employee. Rather, you want your company to be proud that you are their representative both in what you say and do. Your words and actions are just as important to being "on brand" as how you present yourself. More times than I would like to admit, I have worked with companies and HR teams that have had to fire someone because they did something that was not aligned with the core values of a company or brand.

Professional Dressing

You can typically tell the formality of dress from a company's website. There may even be a dress code or manual you are asked to follow. The most common types of business dress codes are the following:

Corporate: This is the most formal dress code, which typically means suit and tie for men and either a suit or a dress, skirt, or slacks with a blouse for women. Shoes should be either polished leather or similar in formality. Both heels and flats are equally appropriate, but closed-toe is the most formal style of shoe for corporate business. Tights are often added in some corporate environments. If a dress is worn, shoulders should remain covered. A suit is a great look for all genders. Just remember that the darker the suit, the more formal it becomes. Match the formality of what you wear with the corporate environment you are in.

Business Professional: This typically means suit (tie if it's a formal environment) or nice slacks with a button-down shirt and blazer for men and dress, skirt, or slacks with a blouse for women. No matter the gender, I think a nice blazer thrown over whatever it is you are wearing always looks professional.

Business Casual: Pants (jeans, khakis, or similar) with a collared shirt and belt for men and women can wear a less formal dress, skirt, or jeans or slacks with any sweater, blouse, or similar top. Beware that hemlines remain a conservative length no matter what dress code you follow.

Casual: Depending on where you live and your company culture, this may even mean shorts. That being said, in business I always recommend you stick with a collared shirt or blouse that is tucked in.

What to Avoid

Beware of these gender-neutral faux pas below which apply to everyone and are often considered unprofessional or inappropriate in business:

- **Showing too much skin.** Let people focus on your brilliance and nothing else.
- **Flip flops.** Save these for your next vacation.
- **Clothing that's too tight.** If you pull your clothing and it bounces back to your skin, it's likely too tight.
- **Ripped clothing or clothing with holes.** Intentional or not!
- **Ill-fitting clothing.** Tailored clothing is best for business, so make sure it fits your body.
- **Empty belt loops.** If you have belt loops and they are showing, there should be a belt in them.
- **Brown belt/black shoes.** If you are wearing a brown belt, wear brown shoes; same for black.
- **Inappropriate materials.** A linen suit is not as formal as a wool suit, no matter what the color!

- **Big logos.** Logos should be small or nonexistent for the most corporate or professional look.
- **Yellowing of underarms on shirts.** If this is a common issue for you, wear an undershirt.

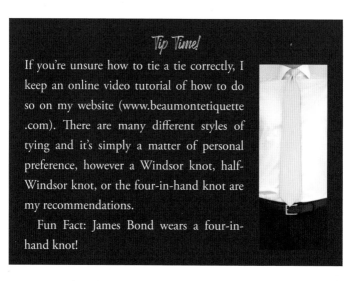

Tip Time!

If you're unsure how to tie a tie correctly, I keep an online video tutorial of how to do so on my website (www.beaumontetiquette .com). There are many different styles of tying and it's simply a matter of personal preference, however a Windsor knot, half-Windsor knot, or the four-in-hand knot are my recommendations.

Fun Fact: James Bond wears a four-in-hand knot!

Dress Code Cheat Sheet

If you are attending an event on behalf of your company, it's important to know how to dress for the occasion, as you are representing your company as well as yourself. Following is a cheat sheet of what to wear for every occasion.

Dress Code	Guidelines for Men's Fashion	Guidelines for Women's Fashion
White Tie	Black dress coat with tails, a white shirt, waistcoat, and bow tie	Floor-length gown, long gloves (optional)
Black Tie	Tuxedo with bow tie or necktie	Floor-length gown
Black Tie Optional	Tuxedo or dark suit with necktie; pocket squares are a bonus!	Floor-length, tea-length, or cocktail dress
Cocktail	Suit with jacket; For formal locations add necktie	Suit or mid-length dress or skirt/pants
Business	Suit with jacket and necktie	Suit or mid-length dress or skirt/pants and top with sleeves (capped to wrist-length)
Business Casual	A tucked-in collared shirt with slacks or jeans (no rips)	Day dress, slacks/skirt with top, jeans (no rips)
Casual	Slacks, jeans (no rips); a button-down shirt or polo; avoid sportswear	Day dress, skirt, slacks, jeans (no rips); avoid athleisure wear

Professional Grooming

Clean-cut and polished is always a good look. Whether you have long, short, or no hair, what matters is that you keep it clean and well-groomed. Facial hair in business can also look very professional if groomed accordingly. Choosing a hairstyle that keeps hair out of your face allows people to see you clearly and is deemed professional. Beware of dandruff, which is the most common issue with hair that

I see. White flakes on a dark suit is never a good look, and dandruff can easily be solved with over-the-counter hair products. Also remember to never groom yourself in the workplace. If you need to comb your hair, etc., do it in private at home or in the bathroom.

Fragrance

I personally never wear fragrance in business and, generally speaking, advise my clients to do the same. A scent you like may not appeal to others in your office and can be a distraction. If you do wear a fragrance, just make sure to spray directly on your skin instead of your clothing, where the scent may stick or be altered by the chemicals in the materials. We put fragrance on our skin's pulse points because that is where heat radiates and causes the scent to activate.

Deodorant

Unless it's for a religious reason, you should always wear lightly scented deodorant. I can't tell you the amount of times an HR team has called my office saying they didn't know how to handle telling someone they had bad body odor. Avoid the uncomfortable situation for everyone and wear it. At my office I keep an emergency supply cabinet for my team that is filled with all kinds of amenities they may need or have forgotten, from sewing kits, Band-Aids, and travel deodorants to breath fresheners and stain wipes.

Nails

A manicure is gender-neutral and everyone in business should make sure their nails are clean, filed, or neatly cut and that their cuticles are taken care of. If you wish to wear polish, in formal corporate environments I recommend sticking to either neutral shades or shades of garden roses. In some service environments, companies may ask that you wear no nail-polish and is a matter of that company's policy.

Skin/Makeup

Your skin should be clean and fresh-looking. If you wear makeup, make sure to keep your personal presentation professional. Your makeup should not be the first thing people notice when they look at you. If you've been using the same skin care products or makeup for more than three years, I recommend going to a skin care or makeup counter to have them rematch your products to your skin. Our skin changes both in texture and color as we age, so the products you been using for five years may not be the best ones for you anymore.

Breath

Especially if you're in a client-facing industry, bad breath can break a business relationship. I recommend always having breath fresheners on you in case a sudden case of bad breath hits. I prefer breath strips instead of mints because the crunching sound can bother other people. Gum in business is never a good idea—it's a major distraction and seen as unprofessional.

Showing Respect in Business Settings

As society evolves, etiquette must evolve with it. The business world has changed drastically in recent years, one example being that of gender in the workplace. Nowadays, it's crucial in Western business that all genders are treated equally, paid equally, and given the same opportunities. I created a modern code of conduct called the Elevator Rules of Business Etiquette to show respect according to nothing else other than rank in business.

Knowing your Rank

When you were young, I bet you were taught to respect elders, give up your seat for someone who needs it, and never talk back to those who have paved the way for us, right? In a business context, the highest-ranking person should get the most respect. No matter the size of a company, it's very important to recognize seniority. Below is a general ranking of titles to help you understand how the majority of companies are structured. Of course, there are many different variations of these titles which may vary depending on the workplace:

Corporate Ladder

- President/CEO (Chief Executive Officer)
- CMO/COO /CFO (Chief Marketing/Operations/Financial Officer)
- SVP (Senior Vice President)
- VP (Vice President)
- Director
- Manager
- Associate/PA (Personal Assistant)
- Junior Associate
- Intern

Elevator Rules of Business Etiquette

Who holds the door open? Who pays the bill at a business lunch? Who holds the elevator door or walks first? Outdated etiquette rules used to say gender dictated the answer to all of these questions, but today it's very important to recognize that gender plays no role. Instead, the answer to these questions raises another one: Who wants to show respect in each situation?

Opening Doors

The golden rule here is that the person wanting to show respect is the one who opens the door. For example, if two female professionals from the same company are walking out of a building, who should open the door in this situation? The woman who is more junior in rank should be handling the door and walking out after the more senior woman. As I am often hosting clients, no matter the gender of the client, I always walk to the door first and open it, gesturing with my hand to say "Please, after you." Even as a woman hosting a group of male clients, I would offer to hold the door open for them, as I would want to show respect to my clients regardless of gender.

Who Orders First?

This is typically dictated by the restaurant service staff who likely have a standard way of taking orders (in the Western world, you will find most servers take the orders of females followed by males). That being said, if you are hosting a mixed-gendered group of clients for a meal, and the server comes to you to order first (no matter your gender), while you should order the wine for the table, when it comes time to order meals, you should always gesture to the highest-ranking woman at the table to order first and say "Please, after you."

Who Pays?

The host is the person who pays. In almost any instance I can think of in business, a client should never pay. You as the host should always pay unless a client has, for instance, invited you as a guest to their holiday dinner party or other special gathering.

Elevator Etiquette

When hosting clients or walking through an elevator with someone ranked higher than yourself, you are in charge of walking ahead to the elevator and pushing the button to call it to your floor. When the door opens, you should be standing to the outside of the elevator door so that you can put your arm out to hold the door open and say "Please, after you." Once everyone has walked through the door, you would follow through after. When you arrive at your floor, hold your arm out again to show that you are keeping the door open for them as they depart the elevator. Only once everyone is out, you would release the elevator door and follow behind.

Revolving Door Etiquette

The amount of times I get this question means it deserves to be addressed! The host is the one who should push the revolving door through. If I'm walking through the revolving door at The Plaza Hotel to take my clients to a dining etiquette lesson, this means that I am the host in charge of taking care of them. Therefore, in order to show respect, I would be the one pushing the revolving door for them. There are two options that are technically correct, but I will tell you which option I prefer and why.

Option 1 (my preferred option): You walk up to the revolving door and with your right hand you start pushing the door gently while with your left hand you gesture to your guest to please walk through while saying "Please, after you." Then, as they walk through, you walk in the revolving door after them and continue to push the heavy weight of the door so you are taking the brunt of the work and not your guest.

Option 2: You immediately walk through the revolving door. Then, when you get through to the other side, you stop and continue pushing the door around until your guest makes it through the door. Then, you walk off together. This option is risky because it can look like an afterthought that you walked through the door first before considering your client.

Did You Know?

The phrase "ladies first" is often synonymous with etiquette. It used to be used to verbally signal a woman to go first ahead of her male counterparts. Instead, now I recommend you simply say "after you" if you'd like someone to walk ahead of you or order ahead of you at a restaurant. With modern etiquette, specifically in business, this phrase is considered outdated and I no longer recommend using it because there is no need to point out or treat genders differently in business.

Headshots

According to a LinkedIn article called "Picture Perfect: Make a Great First Impression with Your LinkedIn Profile Photo," members with a photo receive far more engagement: twenty-one times more profile views and nine times more connection requests. That being said, I would not recommend putting your photo on a résumé, also called a curriculum vitae (CV), as it may imply that you are trying to use your looks to get an interview and may be seen as unprofessional. So, what makes a good headshot? The best profile photos are headshots that show subjects who are:

- Dressed appropriately for the role
- Wearing attire that flatters their body, in colors that complement hair and skin tone; avoiding busy textures, patterns, or logos
- Smiling with the eyes to appear approachable and confident
- Making eye contact with the camera
- Wearing minimal jewelry
- Avoiding direct sunlight, shadows, and fluorescent lighting
- Not cropping out your head or body from a group photo
- Using a solid, bright background color; avoiding white in most cases
- Standing with your body in a three-quarters angle to the camera, placing one foot slightly ahead with hands clasped loosely in front of you
- Capturing waist-up or mid-chest up (avoiding head-only and full body images)
- Applying the rule of thirds in the shot composition to make it more interesting; the subject should stand to the left or right a bit rather than dead center

Technical Tips

- Make sure the photo is in full focus
- Opt for a square image, although this can be cropped at time of upload
- The image should be about 400px x 400px
- The file size limit is about 8MB

Posture and Deportment

The way you sit, stand, and move in business shows others that you are powerful, poised, and confident. Whether you are at a boardroom table or walking to lunch, a few points about posture should always be practiced. To start, there are three cornerstones of posture: chin, shoulders, and legs. Make sure to roll your shoulders back, and keep your chin level so that it is parallel to the floor at all times. A chin that points upward implies that you're daydreaming or even arrogant, and a chin that points down implies indifference or insecurity. Your legs, especially when sitting, are also important and can help you look polished and well-balanced, which in turn makes you look controlled and self-assured.

Sitting Posture

I often hear that good posture while sitting is the most difficult to maintain, because we tend to relax after just a few minutes, curving our spines to find comfort, ultimately slouching. Practice the following tips when sitting to maintain excellent posture:

1. Avoid using armrests. The moment you use armrests, you slowly start to relax and your spine begins to curve.

2. Your back should not be touching the back of the chair. You may have to adjust yourself if a chair has a deeper seat, which is perfectly fine. Imagine you have about the width of a golf ball or egg from the back of your tailbone to the back of the chair. By not leaning backward and resting your back in your chair, you tend to keep a straighter spine when sitting.

3. If you put your hands between your torso and the table you are sitting at, you want to be sure that you are at least 1–1.5 hand's

width away from the table in front of you. You never want your belly touching the table so it appears that you are leaning or hovering over the table or desk.

4.   Remember, no elbows on the table . . . ever. Not at a desk, dinner table, or boardroom table.

While I love teaching modern etiquette in a gender-neutral way, for anatomical reasons on this next lesson, I would suggest the below options for sitting. One thing to note is that no matter your gender, if you cross your legs, make sure that the bottom of your shoe faces down and not toward the people you are interacting with. The reasoning is because you want to keep the bottom of the shoe, which is potentially dirty, not facing your companion. One other point for everyone when you are sitting is to be cautious of movement and fidgeting of your arms, legs and shaking of feet, as it can make you look anxious or bored. Beware of swivel chairs that people often spin or turn from side to side in and can cause you to look unfocused and unprofessional.

Ladies

The sitting positions on the next page have been long practiced by some of the most elegant and powerful women on earth. I recommend any of the below sitting positions. Try them out to find the position that is most comfortable for you. The common denominator of all of my favorite sitting positions is that even when crossed at the knee, your knees and ankles are together.

Four Suggested Sitting Positions

Gents

Gentlemen, try placing your legs hip-width apart and heels firmly planted on the floor. Be careful not to spread your legs so wide that your knees and legs go into someone else's personal space.

Punctuality

This is one of the most age-old and always-in-style points of business etiquette. Being on time tells the person or people you are meeting that you respect their schedules. Being late shows a lack of consideration for other people and can be very frustrating if you are on the receiving end of a late business companion. This also goes for conference calls, group chats, and Skype meetings. If you are going to an interview or a business meeting with an outside client or organization, I recommend showing up ten minutes ahead of the appointment time. You may think it would look more organized to show up earlier than that, but I would avoid doing so, as it causes the person you're meeting to feel rushed to meet with you if they get a buzz from their assistant saying an appointment is twenty minutes early. If it's someone internally at your company who has asked for a meeting, you can show up to the meeting room on the dot of the time of the requested meeting. If you're ever invited to a colleague's home for something like a holiday party, and the invitation says 7:00 p.m., this is when you should never arrive even one moment early, as it's a private home and you may catch your host still preparing. For a private home, I recommend showing up about ten minutes after the start time and always with a host gift in hand. For a larger business networking event or cocktail party, it is acceptable to arrive fifteen to twenty minutes *max* after the invitation time, but remember that the best networking happens early on. "Fashionably late" doesn't apply in business!

Tip Time!

What do you do if you're running late and it is out of your hands? Follow the Meier Method for running late, which is for every minute you think you are going to be late, give two minutes' notice. For example, if you are stuck in traffic and think you are going to be ten minutes late to a business lunch, you should give twenty minutes' notice if possible.

Chapter 2

Effective Communication

Effective communication is one of my favorite topics to instruct because it goes way beyond simple body language tips. When you know how to read someone, you then know how to react to get the most out of your interaction. Whether it's via email, phone, or in-person, becoming an effective communicator in business is crucial to your success.

Always Say Yes to the Water!

It usually takes a few minutes for people to acclimate to a new environment and a new person. When you walk into someone's office, sometimes you will be offered a glass of water and you should say yes! It helps both you and the person offering a moment to relax and acclimate before you jump into the meeting. Water is also great to have if you get nervous. Make sure you take at least a sip or two so it looks natural and don't ask for it and then just let it wastefully sit there untouched. If you are in an interview or when you are trying to win someone else over, I would advise not asking for a coffee or tea, as the person has to prepare it and you may put them out by doing so, even if they offered. (Catch-22, I know.)

In-Person, Phone, and Video Interactions

Whether you are hosting a meeting at your office or attending one at someone else's, there is an unsaid code of conduct that should always be followed. Even if you're not the one in a meeting but you know your company is hosting clients, you should take on the same energy and polish as your colleagues who are attending. When your office is hosting a meeting, be aware of the following:

- Always dress in a manner that represents the company
- Maintain an organized and clean office area
- Make sure any confidential papers, such as client contracts, are out of sight
- Keep your personal phone out of sight
- Be aware of personal space between you and others; don't wander to places you are not invited
- Your appearance, behavior, and volume

When you're attending a meeting at someone else's office, be aware of the following:

- Keep your personal phone out of sight
- Never bring your own coffee or drink to someone else's office; it creates garbage when you leave
- Be aware that you are being observed at all times when with a client
- Everything you say should remain professional not only in the meeting but also in the lobby, reception area, and restrooms. Even in elevators or when you have left the floor of the office you were visiting, you're still on their turf and anything you say or do *can* be held against you!

This last point leads me to a story about why it's important to always remain professional in the workplace. My colleagues and I were scheduled to give a business etiquette presentation at a company in New York City. The building was a skyscraper in Manhattan and had so many floors that there were separate elevator banks for different levels. There were restaurants and coffee shops and even a gift shop that the public was welcome to stroll through before entering the security check for employees, clients, and guests. As my colleagues and I were slightly early for our presentation, we all sat for a coffee. Next to our table were two young, well-dressed men with ties on who were overly excited about their conversation and talking quite loudly. Without trying, my team and I could overhear their entire conversation. They were talking about their wild weekend at the beach, and our eyes widened in disbelief at their use of explicit words. Made uncomfortable by much of the language they were using, we decided to pack up and check in to get our security passes.

By the time we checked in, we found ourselves walking right next to the duo from the coffee shop. They had by now put their suit jackets back on and looked like the upstanding gentlemen I was sure they were hired to be. We all got into the same large elevator together and, sure enough, the two men about whom we knew more than we cared to stepped off on the same floor. Suddenly they were perfect gentlemen, opening the glass doors to the lobby for us and all.

Thirty minutes later, I stood on a stage in front of my presentation, overlooking the podium as company attendees streamed in. In a humorous manner, I started with a story of this one time that I was having a coffee before a business etiquette lesson and overheard an extremely unprofessional conversation. I walked the room through what then happened with the elevator and lobby after that. The room hissed and snickered at where the story was heading. I then told everyone that it was in fact the CEO of the entire company who had personally requested I come in to review business etiquette with his team and to offer any feedback I had.

As I told my little story, I never once made eye contact with the two employees in question, but I could feel their eyes burning into mine. I knew that they knew exactly who I was talking about. I never pointed them out to anyone internally or spoke to them directly, as I imagine the fear of that moment alone may have taught them the valuable lesson at hand. They knew their careers could have been gravely affected by my actions, but I simply wanted them to learn for the future. They were my students, after all!

The moral of the story is that you never know who could be listening in or watching. If I were a new client that day, I fear this story would not have ended up as gently for the two of them. We live and we learn, but take a lesson from these two so that you never make the same mistake they did!

Written Communication

When writing an email, formal letter, direct message, or text to a colleague or client, it is very important to ensure that your copy is grammatically correct as well as spell-checked. Don't be afraid to ask someone to review something you've written if you're unsure about any of the wording. And always remember to be professional no matter which method of communication you're using. If you're sending a formal letter, one suggested format can be found below. Note that written sign-offs can be similar to that of digital sign-offs (page 50), but it's important to still sign your name with an actual written signature, even if it is a typed letter.

Example:

Company Logo (or name)

Name
Title
Company Name
Company Address

Date

Dear _____,

(Body copy not indented) _____

_____

_____

_____

_____

_____

_____

_____

_____

Best regards,

Your Signature Here

Your full name
Your title

Email Communication

Because my team gets so many questions about email etiquette, and it's so important to both our clients and the companies we work with, I've listed the most common email etiquette questions we are asked in regard to business:

Q: Who goes in the CC line?

A: CC means carbon copy. You add a recipient to the CC line of an email so that they can see it for reference and know that the email is not directly addressed to them. For instance, if you are writing to Gordon, the CEO of a company, and you want to keep his assistant Joseph on the email for reference, you would put Gordon's email in the recipient line and Joseph's email in the CC line. Then, you would only address Gordon in the email.

Q: Is there an order of whose email is put first in the recipient line when writing a group email?

A: Yes! You always put the most senior name/email first, followed by any other emails in order of rank. When you address people in the email, names are also in order of rank. For example, if you are emailing a client that is a director level (Irene) and her more junior associate (Deborah), you would put the director's email first, followed by the junior associate. In the email, you would address Irene first, then Deborah, in the order of their rank.

Q: When should I BCC someone?

A: If Dr. Shane sends an email referring me to another specialist, Dr. Bron, when I reply to Dr. Shane, I would say thank you for referring me and that I was moving him to BCC. Then, I would begin speaking directly to Dr. Bron in the email. It's important if someone introduces you to another person in an email that they don't get stuck in a long spiral of emails that may clog their inbox.

Q: How long should an email be?
A: After two paragraphs, I tend to start skimming emails. Therefore, I recommend keeping emails as short as possible to keep the recipient's attention. If you have actionable items or points you want to draw specific attention to, include a few bullets that stand out in the body of the email. Always include next steps in an email if possible.

Q: Are there any rules about images or attaching them?
A: If you are attaching files or images, make sure the file names are professional and clearly label what is in the file.

Q: Can I use acronyms or "text" language in emails?
A: Avoid using acronyms in formal emails. Acronyms like "ASAP" should be written out as "as soon as possible" instead.

Q: Do I have to spell all words out or can I use symbols like the "&" symbol?
A: It can be seen as lazy and unprofessional to include symbols rather than spelling words out. When in doubt, skip the shortcut and spell it out!

Q: What makes a good subject line of an email?
A: Short, concise, and to the point! Avoid capitalizing every letter and using punctuation in subject lines.

Q: What are the proper salutations to start off a formal email in business?

A: "Dear XX," "Good morning," "Good afternoon," or "Good evening" are all appropriate greetings.

Q: What are the proper closings to sign off a formal email in business?
A: "Best regards," is the most professional closing. Suggested alternatives, depending on your relationship, personality, or industry also include but are not limited to "With regards," "Kind regards," "Warmest regards," and "With best wishes,".

Q: Do I have to keep being formal in my opening greeting if the email has been going back-and-forth multiple times in communication?
A: No. After the first couple of emails back-and-forth, a formal greeting may start to come across as unnatural. After I have spoken in an email chain a few times, I tone down the formality a bit and stop using Dear/Good morning, etc. and instead, depending on the conversation, just jump into the email. For instance, after three to four emails I may start an email with "Thank you, Karen. That sounds fantastic and I look forward to meeting with you tomorrow. Best regards, Myka."

Q: How do I address a large team on an email?
A: For informal groups or emails you can say "Dear all," or for formal groups or emails you can keep it to "Good morning," etc., as that would cover addressing everyone.

Q: What does a professional signature look like in an email?
A: Your company may have a standard signature they'd like you to use. If they don't, and you're creating your own signature, there is no exact formula, but here are some basic examples:

Corporate signature:	**Business (informal) signature:**
Valentina LaMont	Valentina LaMont
Associate	Associate
XYZ Consulting	(m) 1-917-555-0187
123 Fifth Avenue	(o) 1-212-555-0100
New York, New York 10019	@socialmediahandle
1-212-555-0100	
www.xyz.com	

Surprising Language **Not** to Use in an Email and Why

1. "As discussed," can come across as condescending. "In regard to points X, Y, Z . . ." is more appropriate.

2. "No problem" is a problem! As it's hard to read someone's tone in an email, responding to someone's request with these two words could be taken as you having an attitude.

3. Don't start off a formal email with "Hello" or "Hi." It's too familiar to use such informal wording for a formal introduction. Instead, stick with my suggested salutations above.

4. Don't ever send internal-only images and documents. You could lose your job for sending internal-only files and imagery. Remember there is a reason it was classified for company use only!

5. Always ask someone before you forward their email. When people write emails to one another, it's based on their relationship with the person they are communicating with. Sometimes informal communication intended for one person would never be appropriate to send to another. For this reason, you should never forward someone else's email to another person without asking the person first.

6. Beware of capitalization and exclamation marks. The tone of an email is arguably one of its most important elements. Putting words IN ALL CAPS implies that you are shouting. Exclamation points may show excitement, but they can also show anger or unhappiness, and using too many of them in a business email is generally viewed as unprofessional.

7. Don't include emojis in formal business emails. Socially it's fine to text and email whatever emojis make you happy, but not in business. I advise not including emojis in work emails, as this is often seen as unprofessional.

Clear, Concise, and Effective Nonverbal Communication Skills

The best communicators in business are typically the best professionals and the most successful at what they do because of how they respond to a tricky situation, defuse a tense moment, or make people feel understood. While we can't help what people say or do, we can help our reactions. According to Albert Mehrabian, a pioneer researcher of body language, the total impact of a message is about 7 percent verbal (words only), 38 percent vocal (tone of voice, inflection, and other sounds) and 55 percent nonverbal (body movements, facial expressions, energy). It's almost startling to think of physical actions speaking louder than words . . . quite literally. Mastering nonverbal communication is key for successful conversations and interactions in business.

Reading Facial Expressions . . . and Why It's So Important!

Great communicators know that when a person is angry, upset, happy, confused, or content, their reaction to that person is a crucial next step in a successful interaction. I'm going to teach you how to read a person's facial expression by identifying two easy points on their face. This is a crucial skill set in business. Once you can read faces like a pro, you'll know how to respond in any situation.

The secret is when someone is listening to you, watch their eyes and mouth together. What these two parts of the face are doing at the same time tells you how to respond. For example, if you are giving a sales pitch to someone and they are pinching their mouth and their eyes at the same time, you know they are likely not on board with whatever you're selling. This tells you to change strategy or the angle in which you are selling, and fast! Look at the following series of facial expressions. Even without knowing what the conversation is about or any words being said, we can easily recognize someone's thoughts.

Eyes pinched and mouth pinched = skeptical/unsure/distrusting

Eyes pinched and mouth open = thinking/interested/digesting information

Eyes open and mouth open = understanding/interested/engaged

Eyes open and mouth pinched = skeptical/unsure/distrusting

Head Nod

Head nods are a great form of nonverbal communication to see from someone you are speaking with. By nodding their head in conversation, the other person is expressing that they are on board with you and agreeing with what you are saying. If you are speaking to someone else and you want to show receptiveness, it's important for you to also gently nod your head as a nonverbal sign to show that you are listening to what they are saying.

Bad Etiquette

How should you handle bad etiquette? If you are with a client or colleague who is always showing bad etiquette, or maybe you see them reach for the wrong fork at dinner, the correct thing to do is ignore it! Correcting bad etiquette *is* bad etiquette. The exception is if you are a manager, HR person, or managing a team. If fact, if this is the case, then it's actually up to you to help fix the issue at hand or report it to the appropriate department to mediate or train the person/team at hand.

Confrontation

Diplomats are chosen to represent a country abroad mainly for their soft skills. You would never send an overly aggressive personality into another country to strengthen relations. If you find yourself in a tense situation or confrontation, here are a few points to remember on how to always come across as polite yet firm and assertive.

Don't Let It Boil Over

If you have an issue with someone, like a colleague, don't let it get worse and worse until you are so angry you can't think straight. Don't let your frustrations hit the boiling point. Instead, address the issue upfront and politely, and have a suggested solution ready.

Think before You Speak or Write

Never write, text, or email someone when you are angry. You can draft it, but don't send it. Wait until things cool down, reread it, and then edit it once you are more levelheaded. Remember that anything in writing can come back to haunt you, so do so with caution!

Passive-Aggressive Behavior Rarely Works in Business

Passive-aggressive behavior is one of the most common pet peeves in business. An example of passive-aggressive behavior in an office environment would be someone that answers with "fine" or "I don't care" when you can read between the lines that they are not fine or that they really do care. Another less obvious example would be the way you work with others: "Sarah, do you think we should have the project finished within the hour?" If you know it's due at that time. Instead, an example of what could be a more constructive way of working together would be: "Sarah, our presentation is due in an hour. What can I do to help make sure we meet the deadline?"

Never Raise Your Voice

Nothing good can come out of fighting fire with fire when it comes to constructive communication in business. If someone such as a boss, colleague, or client is angry with you and raising their voice, for you to raise your voice back is the worst thing you can do. Instead, keep your cool, remain poised, and answer with a firm yet assertive voice. If the person is too hotheaded to listen at that moment, let them cool off and pick up the conversation when the situation has calmed down.

Cross-Cultural Etiquette

Always follow the etiquette and protocol of the country and culture you are in. For example, if the Duke and Duchess of Cambridge came to America, the President and First Lady of the United States would not curtsey or bow, because that is not how we greet people in America. If you are traveling to another country for business it's crucial to do your research ahead of time to understand everything from basic greetings to dining and even religion (some religions do not allow you to physically touch). Incorrect etiquette can make or break a business deal in a foreign country. While this book only covers Western business etiquette, you can also learn international etiquette for a number of countries from my company by special request or through a number of online resources.

Tip Time!

Always remember that ethnic restaurants are like mini embassies. To show respect, you would therefore adopt the cultural etiquette of the restaurant when you enter. For example, when I go to a Japanese restaurant, I will use the chopsticks they provide, as it's their culture to eat with them.

Perfecting Your Voice in Business

It's crucial to have a strong, unwavering voice in business. From how fast you speak, to your tone, having the right balance takes practice. It's important to identify if you have areas to work on, and if so, to tackle them. The most common issues are:

- Speaking too fast or slow.
- Speaking too loud or soft.
- Ending sentences with your voice going up to a squeaky pitch or ending sentences with your voice trailing off at the end.
- Speaking in a monotone voice. You want to show two points of inflection in every sentence to show maximum engagement (especially if you're going into sales or if you'll be speaking on the phone a lot).
- Speaking too much and not letting others speak or speaking over others.
- Using filler words. I find the most common are: um, ah, like, so, and okay.
- Using slang verbiage. Instead of using "yeah," use "yes."
- Swearing. It's not professional and may show a lack of education.

Public Speaking

According to a Chapman University study on fears in America, a fear of public speaking is America's biggest phobia, with 25.3 percent of people saying they have a fear of speaking in front of a crowd. I used to share this fear until I learned some easy-to-practice tips. Now, after years of practice, I feel comfortable and confident giving presentations and instructing crowds of over one thousand people at a time. Here are my top tips to help with public speaking:

Prepare: Practice your presentation so you are not reading from a screen or note cards. The better you know the material, the more confident you will appear when you present it.

Know your audience: Adjust your presentation to be the most engaging for your specific audience. Sometimes I need to present to a serious group of attorneys and other times a casual group of tech marketers. My presentation style would be drastically different for each group. Research your audience before you present. Even for small groups of people in a room, I always make sure to make eye contact with as many people in the room as possible, so they all feel like I'm connecting with them and it becomes more personal. If you are in a large audience with lights shining on you so you can't see individual eyes, make sure you have a few points throughout the room in all directions you look at throughout your lecture or presentation so you can engage with the audience.

Turn nerves into excitement! Remember that your audience is sitting and waiting to listen to you because you are knowledgeable on a topic that they are interested in. Have confidence in knowing they are there to see you and hear you and get excited. When my nerves get the best of me, I have been known to do jumping jacks backstage!

Use your tools: Think about what tools you will have while you're presenting and make sure you are comfortable using them. Will you have a handheld microphone or an earpiece? Do you have a remote to click through your presentation? Will you have a podium to put your laptop on? The more visual aids you have, the better. I always like to see a room before I present in it whenever possible. I like to sit in a room before I present, too, so that by the time I get up to present, I am much more acclimated to the group I will be addressing. Make sure to always do a sound check before you get up to speak!

Breathe deep: The more oxygen your brain and body receive, the calmer you'll feel.

I'd like to introduce you to a simple yet powerful method that renowned Harvard-trained physician Dr. Shane Volncy teaches his patients, called the 5 x 5 breathing exercise, a technique that can help instantly activate the parasympathetic nervous system, which controls our body's ability to relax. This technique forces both the mind and body to relax and concentrate on regulating the breath, rather than focusing on your nerves. This simple breathing method can act as a "natural relaxant for the nervous system." How it works: Begin by standing or sitting up straight, relax your neck and shoulders, and breathe in slowly for five seconds through your nose, focusing on the sensation that you feel as the air runs through your nose, down your throat, and deep into your chest. Then, blow out through your mouth slowly five seconds. I do this for two to three minutes about five minutes before I go on stage or feel nervous.

Tip Time!

The larger the crowd, the less responsive they tend to be, as crowds typically feel they are less accountable for reacting when many others are there. This means that the faster you can warm them up, the better. I always start my speeches or presentations with a little humor or warmth when I am speaking to larger groups. For very large groups, think of the speaking area as a stage where your reactions, facial expressions, and words need to be a little bit larger as would be the same for a Broadway performer. Make sure not to stay glued to a podium. Don't be afraid to walk around the stage, but don't pace back and forth like a lion.

Chapter 3

Technology Etiquette

Technology has changed the way we do almost everything from communicating (see chapter 2 on page 43) to applying for jobs to managing our finances. And with these new tools literally at our fingertips come a wide range of etiquette guidelines that should be followed. As technology evolves, these guidelines will change, but we will always keep in mind that above all else, they are in place to assist in how these tools should be used, navigated, and how to respect others through their use.

Sending and Receiving Emails

The following are the do's and don'ts to keep in mind when sending and receiving emails.

- To the best of your ability, reply to all work emails within the day you received the message, or at least within twenty-four hours if it was received late in the day.
- When you click reply to an email with multiple addresses, make sure you're not replying all by mistake.
- Spelling and grammar are both extremely important. Don't rely on spell-check alone to confirm that you haven't made any mistakes in the body of your email. Spell-check won't be able to tell you if you used the wrong version of your (versus you're) or there (versus their or they're), so double-

check everything before you press send, as glaring typos and misspellings can come across as careless and inattentive.

- Be respectful of other people's inboxes and don't forward chain emails.

Landlines versus Mobile Phones

Don't be afraid of a landline phone. Many young people aren't used to communicating over a phone and are more comfortable with texting, emails, and direct messages, but in an office setting it's not always possible to ignore the phone on your desk.

A cell phone at the office can be a distraction to both yourself and those around you. Keep your ringer on vibrate so if it does ring you don't interrupt your colleagues. Also, if you receive consistent notifications, you may find yourself constantly reaching for your phone to check them. Keep your phone out of sight during the day unless you're expecting an emergency call.

Landline Etiquette

- Decide on a friendly greeting to use each time you answer your phone, such as "Good morning, how may I help you?" or "The Smith Company, this is Jane." Your company may also recommend a specific greeting.
- Don't shout into the phone. The person on the other end will be able to hear you at normal volume. Have your ringer volume set at a medium level to avoid bothering your colleagues.
- Your office phone should have a custom voice mail message with a greeting letting the caller know they reached the right person. Be sure to check your voice mails before the end of the day and return any missed calls.

- Avoid leaving someone on hold for more than a few minutes. If you know that you need to address another issue before speaking to them, ask if you can call them back and when they are available to speak with you later in the day.

Cell Phone Etiquette

- Turn your cell phone to silent or vibrate in a business setting, including meetings and with clients.
- If you need to take a call while with clients or colleagues, excuse yourself and step away from the group or table.
- If you are expecting a call while in a meeting or at a meal with clients or colleagues, inform the people you are with that you are expecting a call.
- Never put your phone on a dining table in formal dining unless it's been noted as a working lunch.
- Avoid talking on your cell phone while riding in an elevator.
- Only use your "work" phone for business purposes.

Hear This About Headphones

Take your headphones or earbuds off if you're not using them. Your colleagues can't tell that you're not listening to anything and may not want to interrupt you. It may be seen as a sign of disrespect to have your headphones in while talking to someone as it gives the impression that you are not fully paying attention to the conversation.

Sending and Receiving Money

It's not uncommon to owe a colleague money for ordering lunch, but it's important to pay them back as soon as possible. No one likes to be out of pocket, and having to ask people repeatedly to pay you back puts everyone in an uncomfortable situation. If you do not have cash on you, it's quick and easy to send someone money via financial apps. If you're the one who is owed money, it's okay to send a request via a financial app if a mention in-person or over email doesn't do the trick.

Being Social on Various Media

Even with privacy settings, it is still possible for employers, potential employers, and recruiters to view your personal social media profiles and gauge whether you're a good fit for the company. People have been passed over for jobs as well as let go from companies for inappropriate content they post on social media. It's important to understand that as a representative of the company you work for, the company will want to ensure your posts don't go against the company's values. A general rule to follow is if you wouldn't want your parents or future boss to see or read what you've posted, don't post it at all. Keep an eye on what other people post about you as well. When you're tagged in a photo, if you don't like that it was posted, it's okay to ask that it be taken down.

Here's a story shared with me by a client who found an employee's troubling social media page. My client had hired a number of graduates from a well-respected business school. After a few months had passed, the company discovered that one of their newly hired employees was posting pictures that included the use of illegal drugs, as well as sexualized images of both men and women. The photos were on multiple public social networks that included the name of the company he worked for. The Human Resources team along with his direct manager determined that these images were not just inappropriate but were also a negative reflection on the company. The company decided to fire the employee based on his posts and for breaking the code of conduct he signed upon his hiring.

Post with Caution

You can be reprimanded or even fired for sharing offensive content, even if you weren't the one who created it. Think twice before reposting or copy and pasting publicly available material, because it may cost you your position.

Link in to Colleagues, Friends, and Associates on LinkedIn

Unlike other social networks, LinkedIn is specifically for professional use. Highlighting your career, updating contacts with articles you've written or were featured in, and interacting with those in your industry are all beneficial for growing professionally. Human resources professionals and recruiters as well as those looking for specialists will turn to LinkedIn to find new talent, so it's important that you put your best foot forward in several ways.

Headshots

Your LinkedIn headshot should be a professional-looking one where you are looking at the camera and are the only person in the photo. Turn back to page 36 to learn how to take a great headshot.

Your Résumé

You can copy and paste your résumé content into your LinkedIn profile, but since you're not limited to one or two pages of paper, you can elaborate on what your role was at each position and your accomplishments.

- Don't lie or mislead anyone with your career history. List company names, titles, and dates at each position correctly.
- List all relevant goals and accomplishments.
- Use keywords to ensure that your profile comes up in more searches. Search LinkedIn for the keywords you think are important and see if you're happy with the results you're seeing, then use those words in your own profile when describing past jobs you've held.
- Take advantage of the summary section to sum up what you do and what you're looking to do next. Unlike a brief résumé objective, this section can be several paragraphs long.
- Be careful not to use the same words again and again or use words that aren't impressive. For example, if your first job focused on ordering supplies, write that you "organized and maintained" office supplies, as it sounds more impressive.

Profile Inspiration

It's okay to find inspiration for your profile from other profiles. Don't copy them verbatim, but look to see how someone in a similar position describes their role. It may remind you of a task or responsibility you forgot to add to your own job descriptions.

Recommendations and Endorsements

Be strategic in who you ask to write a recommendation or to endorse you. Ask colleagues, managers, clients, or vendors you've had good relationships with. You can also offer to write a reciprocal one for them.

Creating a Network

LinkedIn was made for networking and it's very easy to find people on the site, but I don't recommend haphazardly requesting everyone the algorithm suggests. Here are my suggestions for building your network.

- Reach out to people you know and who know you: friends, colleagues, managers, and vendors.
- For people you have met but don't have a strong relationship with, or at least not yet, include a message along with your request to remind the person how you met or know one another.
- Be cautious of sending requests to people you don't know on LinkedIn. They can click that they don't know you, and too many of those may raise a red flag on your account.

Settings

Review the setting options for LinkedIn when you sign up or update your account after reading this chapter. You can set your profile to private, which can be helpful if you are looking for a new position but haven't yet left your current one. You can also decide who you want to share updates with.

Sharing News and Updates

Don't be shy about sharing exciting information about yourself, company, and career. If you write an article or story about something industry related, post it! If you are quoted or featured in an article or story, share that link! It's perfectly acceptable to highlight your career milestones on LinkedIn.

Chapter 4

Client Hosting and Entertaining

Meeting with clients and important guests, such as government officials, requires the utmost level of hospitality and service, not just in a presentation but in how they are greeted and treated throughout their visit. Client and VIP meetings can happen at the office, but they can also happen at an off-site location, such as a restaurant, bar, or industry or social event. It's very important that even though you are not at the office you still behave as the host and ensure your guest is comfortable and happy. If the restaurant makes a mistake on your guest's lunch order, it won't be your fault, but if you spend more time on your phone than with the client you could lose their business permanently. If you are not sure how to be the host or hostess with the most in a business setting, here are some tips to keep in mind:

First Impressions

A receptionist is most often the first person a guest will see and meet when they enter a company's office. It's important for the receptionist's desk, and reception area overall, to be neat and organized. The reception area should not be a storage area. Stacks of files and packages should not be kept in the reception area. If there are confidential documents at the receptionist's desk, they should be kept out of sight, especially when he or she has to walk away from their desk.

If the receptionist has to leave the desk, they should have someone they can ask to sit in their chair so that the reception area is not left unattended. There should be no personal items, including mobile phones, out in the open, as this is a very public area.

Greeting Guests

Every guest should feel welcome from the moment they enter the reception area. (There's only so much control a business has over a building lobby if they don't own the building.) When greeting a client, make eye contact and smile. A receptionist should never make someone feel as if they are interrupting them. Create a standard greeting that a receptionist says to all guests. Appropriate formal greetings include "Good morning/good afternoon," "Welcome to (insert company name here)," and "How many I help you?".

For guests who will have to wait for their appointment or meeting, be honest about the delay and keep them updated if their wait time will be extended. Here's how to ensure a guest's comfort at the office:

- Offer them a seat in the reception area or in a conference room if they need to set up a presentation.
- Instead of pointing with your finger, gesture in the direction of the seating area by facing your palm up and directing them to the chairs or sofa.
- Do not send someone to a conference room on their own. Instead, lead them to the correct room and make sure they have everything they need: Wi-Fi details, cords, beverages, etc.
- Offer to take their coat (see how below).
- Offer a drink (see how below).

- Have reading materials, preferably about the company, on a coffee table or reading stand in the reception area. These can include business or industry magazines, the day's newspaper, and/or the company's annual report.
- When walking someone to a meeting room or office, try not to turn your back to them completely. Walk with your torso on the diagonal so you can continue a conversation.
- Open the door and let the guest walk into the room, holding the door open for them.

How to Take Someone's Coat

When someone arrives at your office, offer to take their coat, jacket, umbrella, luggage, etc. When offering to take someone's coat, ask, "Please, can I take your coat?" To take someone's coat, place a coat over your arm. Layering several coats over your arm is acceptable. To help someone remove their coat, pinch the top of the shoulders and pull down, and place the coat over your arm. If a guest is carrying a wet umbrella, offer a wet-umbrella bag or keep an umbrella stand in the reception area. If someone asks if they can leave their coat or belongings in a coat closet, don't point them to the closet. Instead, guide them there and hold the door open for them, or take their things and bring them to the closet yourself.

Beverage Service at the Office

Whether someone is going to be in the office for a quick meeting or a lengthy one, it's appropriate to offer them something to drink. Water, sparkling or still, coffee, tea, or other beverages should be readily available or easy to make in the office kitchen. Each drink is served in a different way. Follow the guidelines below to learn how to correctly serve water, coffee, and tea.

Water

Water should be served in a glass. If a bottle of water is offered, place an empty glass next to it. Water glasses should not have a stem for ease of use. When pouring water into a glass from a bottle, pitcher, or faucet, only fill the glass halfway and not to the rim. When pouring water out of a bottle, pour the water ¾ way up the glass and leave the bottle on the table to refill at their leisure. Place the glass on a coaster or a paper or fabric cocktail-sized napkin. If serving a glass of water with ice, place no more than three cubes in the glass. For an additional touch, have presliced lemon and lime wedges available on a bread plate. Follow the same guidelines for serving soda.

Coffee

Whether you're serving coffee hot or iced, fill the cup or glass three-quarters of the way to leave room for cream or milk. If the guest asks for black coffee, fill the cup slightly higher. When serving espresso, a demitasse cup should be filled halfway and served with a demitasse spoon. A coffee beverage should be served with a teaspoon. The office kitchen or reception area should have a selection of sugars or sweeteners and milk or cream available. Place a cocktail napkin or coaster beneath a coffee mug or iced coffee glass. The handle of a coffee cup or mug should face the 3 o'clock position. When you are refilling a coffee cup, replace the cup after the third refill. For iced coffee, place a wrapped straw next to the glass, not in the glass.

Tea

Offer an assortment of teas: black, green, and herbal. Always ask how strong the guest would like their tea—strong, medium, or weak— and then steep accordingly. If using a teapot with tea bags, remove and discard the tea bag before pouring a cup. If the tea bag will steep in the teacup, place the tea bag in the cup first, then pour the hot water over it. Bring a ramekin and tell the guest that the ramekin is for their tea bag. If using a teapot with loose-leaf tea, you will need to supply individual tea strainers for your guests.

In-Person Meetings

It's important to show supervisors they can trust you with various projects and tasks, which can only be beneficial to you in growing your career. For all scheduled meetings, make sure you know the topic at hand and are equipped to answer any questions, present ideas, and make suggestions to show those in the room that you are a valuable asset to the company. Follow these guidelines to put your best foot forward:

Be Prompt and Prepared

When attending a meeting with colleagues, managers, or clients, it's important to be on time and organized. You may want to arrive a few minutes early, as it will take a little time to become acclimated to the setting. If you think you will be late for a meeting, give everyone two minutes notice for every one minute you will be late. For example, when running five minutes late, tell everyone you're running ten minutes behind so that they aren't left sitting in a room waiting for you or on a call listening to elevator music. If there are empty seats at the table, do not sit in one at the head or in the direct center on either side of the table as those are often reserved for the most senior person in the room (according to job title, not age) or the client, who would be deemed the VIP in the room.

Make sure you come prepared to any meeting you are invited to attend. Coming prepared means doing your homework and knowing about the topic being discussed, especially if you anticipate that you will have to answer questions or make a presentation. Bring a notebook and a pen with you to take notes, or a laptop if that's your preferred form of notetaking. Grab a professional notebook and a pen that works.

Business cards can be brought with you if you are meeting with people from outside the company for the first time. It's customary to pass out or exchange cards at the end of the meeting. When a card is handed to you, accept it in the same style, with one hand or two hands. Look at both the front and back of the card before putting it away.

When taking notes in a notebook, write legibly so not only you, but others can read your handwriting if you need to share them. You may want to devise your own way of organizing your notes. Here's an example:

Holiday Party

- Guest list
  - Employees
  - Employee spouses/partners
  - Client list
- Venue Requirements
  - Fits at least 150 people
  - Exclusive use
- Catering
  - Contact at least 3 companies for RFPs
    - Company 1
    - Company 2
    - Company 3
- Invitations
  - Design with company colors and logo
  - Email only, no printing

If you are going to take notes on your laptop, don't forget to save the file every few minutes so it doesn't get erased by accident.

And just because you have Wi-Fi access on your laptop doesn't mean you should check email or search the Internet unless directed to do so during the meeting.

Avoid taking notes on your cell phone unless you have no choice, and in that case be sure to make it clear that you are taking notes. If it is not made clear that you're taking notes on your cell phone it may be assumed that you are playing a game, checking your Instagram feed, or doing something other than paying attention. Another note on cell phones at meetings: It's not uncommon to bring a mobile phone to a meeting, but avoid checking it constantly. Be sure that the phone is on vibrate or silent. Better yet, press "Do Not Disturb." If an important call or email does come in, excuse yourself and answer it outside the room.

Drinking and Eating

Avoid eating or drinking more than a coffee, tea, or glass of water at a meeting unless it's a "working lunch" meeting. Gauge the group that you're with and time of the meeting. If the meeting is first thing in the morning, several colleagues may bring coffee. If you do decide to bring a meal or snack to a working lunch meeting, bring something that's not too messy and nothing with too powerful a smell. When a client is in the office, be sure to offer them a drink of water, coffee, tea, or another beverage that is readily available. If the meeting will include a celebratory element, such as toasting a new client or goal reached, be sure you have enough glasses, plates, and utensils for everyone.

Conference Calls

When scheduling a conference call, be sure that all parties have the correct phone number or dial-in with access code, or in the case of video, the direct link to access it through a videoconference service.

Phone calls taken in a noisy area can be distracting to others on the call, so when in a loud environment, place yourself on mute. You should also mute yourself if you plan to type on your keyboard, as the rattling of the keys can also be a distraction, and take the call via handset or headset rather than speakerphone. Video calls should be taken in a quiet setting as well. Be sure that the background is clean or at least organized and that you're in quiet space. If you can't reserve a conference room, wear headphones to ensure that you're not disturbing your colleagues with the audio from the call.

Socializing at Networking Events

Drinks after work, industry networking events, and cocktail parties are a good opportunity to connect and foster better relationships with colleagues and clients. It's important to remember that these are still work events, and just because they take place after hours, like a business trip (see Chapter 9 on page 125), doesn't mean you should behave as if this was solely a social gathering of friends.

Drinking

Holding a drink, alcoholic or not, will make you appear more approachable. Hold your drink in your left hand so you can shake hands with your right as you greet others. If your left hand is holding a plate or clutch, you can gently place your glass on top of it, secured with your left thumb so it doesn't fall, and shake hands with your right.

Tip Time!

Never eat a garnish in a drink that has been submerged in the liquid of the beverage. For instance, if a drink has a cherry on a pick, it is fine to eat, however, if it does not and is at the bottom of your drink, do not fish it out to eat!

Know your limit if you decide to have wine, cocktails, or other liquors. This is still a business setting and you don't want to behave in a manner that can embarrass you or the company. Set your own drink limit and stick to it. And don't forget to eat something.

Finger Foods

Most food at networking events and cocktail parties can be eaten without utensils, but there's still a correct way to eat them. Bar snacks include pretzels, nuts, and olives. Don't eat them directly out of the communal bowl. Place the food on your cocktail napkin or a plate before putting them in your mouth. Canapés are bite-sized menu items, also referred to as hors d'oeuvres, that may be passed around by servers or displayed on a buffet. Before picking up food, take a napkin from the server or a plate from a buffet, and place each piece of food on it before eating it. If there is a dip, scoop a spoonful onto the lower right area of your plate. Limit the number of pieces you take of an item no matter how much you like it to leave enough for everyone to enjoy. Stick with items that can be eaten in one or two bites so you can take a bite and keep up with a conversation. Avoid foods that are greasy, flaky or difficult to eat or manage.

Chapter 5

Networking

No matter what industry you're in, it's highly likely that you will spend some time at a networking event. These events may be run by the company you work for, a trade organization, or even someone simply trying to connect different individuals. Regardless of the host, here are some basic rules to follow in order to put your best foot forward and to ensure that you don't embarrass yourself or the company.

When invited to a networking event, be sure to RSVP by the registration date and read any guidelines posted on the event website or in the confirmation email you receive. There may be instructions as to the attire you should wear, a list of speakers you may want to read up on, and the timing of speeches. While fashionably late is something we've all heard of, I recommend showing up within the first twenty minutes of the event's start time, because the best networking will happen at the beginning of the event before people pair up and group off. Once you arrive, put your cell phone away. You may feel insecure and want to reach for it, but it will instantly make you look unapproachable.

Notes on Networking

The idea of networking can cause stress when the pressure is on to meet new people, but if you forget the "working" part you can focus on what networking truly is all about: relationships. Don't go into a networking event or opportunity with the mind-set of handing out or collecting the most business cards. Focus on connecting with people to forge new relationships that are long-lasting and not simply transactional.

How to Wear a Name Tag

Some events may offer you a preprinted name tag to wear at the event. This is a must, as the whole point of being there is to meet new people and reconnect with familiar faces. If the name tag is on a lanyard, wear it around your neck and make sure that your name is facing people and not mistakenly put on backward. If there is a pocket in the back of your name tag, this is a good place to put some business cards. If your name tag is on a pin or magnet, place it over your heart on your left side so when you extend your right hand to greet people and shake hands the upper part of your right arm doesn't block the tag. If you wear it on your right side, people won't be able to read it as they greet you. When a blank name tag is given to you, write your name so that it is legible and easy to read. Block letters may be a better choice than script for this reason.

What's Your Name Again?

It happens to all of us! You know you have met someone before and you know a number of different details about the person, but for the life of you, you just can't remember their name. Here's what to do so the person you're talking to doesn't realize that you don't remember their name. After you've spoken with them for a few minutes and you are 100 percent sure that you have no idea what their name is, walk them over and introduce them to a friend or colleague by saying, "I'd love for you to meet my colleague, Sam." At this point, Sam will extend his hand for a handshake and introduce himself. "Hi, I'm Sam." And the person you've been speaking with will reciprocate. "Hello, I'm Alice." This is when you would jump into the conversation with, "Alice and I were just talking about . . ." And because it was all done so seamlessly, Alice will never know that you hadn't remembered her name!

Tip Time!

Never tell someone that you "forgot" their name or can't "remember" their name. It's a bit insulting. Instead, ask them to "remind" you of their name if you have only met them that night or one time before.

How and Where to Meet New People

It's not easy going up to strangers and striking up a conversation, but there are some tricks that can help calm your nerves. First, identify who you want to talk to by scanning the room upon your arrival or checking ahead of time if there is a registration of people who will be attending the event. Take a deep breath and walk up and introduce yourself. Don't panic about coming up with something clever to say. Instead, simply start with "Hi, I'd like to introduce myself. My name is John Smith, and I work at (company name)." People are creatures of habit. They tend to choose a specific spot at a networking event where they feel comfortable, and stay in one spot throughout the evening. If you continuously move yourself around the room, introducing yourself to people as you go, you'll find that you're going to meet a lot more people. I suggest you walk counterclockwise around the room. If you're nervous about approaching a group or walking up to someone, place yourself at or near the bar. A lot of people will break off from a group conversation to get another drink on their own. If there is a group of people and you want to speak with someone in the group, look to see if it's an open or closed circle. An open circle will have space for someone to join easily while a closed circle doesn't allow for someone to join the group. Don't squeeze or force yourself into the circle, but wait for an opening when someone steps away.

What to Talk About

You're at a business event, so it would make sense to talk about business-related things, but don't limit the conversation to the state of the company and office news. Have a few other topics prepared that you're knowledgeable about. You should also keep in mind topics that you should steer clear from. You don't want to be the one to start a heated political debate or bring up a taboo topic that you didn't realize was off-limits. You also want to avoid starting a conversation with "So, what do you do?" It can come across as opportunistic, as if you will only talk to the person if you think you can get something out of the conversation. Start on a friendlier note before inquiring about what the person does for work. Don't ever be afraid to start or participate in a conversation, but if you're not sure where to begin, here is a list of topics to bring up or avoid at a networking event. These can apply to other group settings as well!

Bring Up These Topics	Here's Why
Upcoming events such as festivals, concerts, or business conferences	You may find that the people you're talking to have similar interests. Having something in common is a great way to start an ongoing relationship

Bring Up These Topics	Here's Why
Current events	There are plenty of things happening in your local area, the nation, and the world that you can discuss that are not controversial, especially if you've read up on them and can speak knowledgably about them.
Compliments	It's okay to compliment the person you're talking to, but avoid mentioning physical attributes such as what they're wearing. Instead, focus on projects they've worked on, presentations they've made, or other accomplishments.

Avoid These Topics	Here's Why
Politics	A heated political discussion is not appropriate at a business event. Plus, while you may think you know what someone's political leanings are, you may not be correct.
Sex	Whether specifically talking about sex, using the word "sexy" or saying something that may be deemed sexual harassment, it's important to stay away from this topic entirely.
Weather	Except in instances of extreme weather that is currently happening, talking about the weather is both boring and a dead-end conversation.

Avoid These Topics	Here's Why
Family	Unless you know someone's marital status and whether they have children, it is best to steer clear of asking someone specifics about their family like "so are you married?" or "do you have children?" as it may be seen as too personal and may even result in them telling you they are struggling with fertility or going through a divorce.
Illness or Diet	Don't describe the symptoms or side effects of a recent illness you have had or go into detail about what specific diet you are on

Keep the Conversation Going

Now that you've introduced yourself and started chatting with someone or a group of people, how do you keep the conversation going without talking about yourself too much? Ask open-ended questions. I devised the perfect strategy to help you keep the conversation going to ensure that you avoid an awkward silence and an uncomfortable end: The Meier Method W-W-H-C, which stands for What, Why, How, Compliment. Unlike "when," "where," and "who," which can often lead to one-word answers, "what," "why," and "how" are open-ended questions. For example:

Q: Did you go to last month's sales meeting?
A: Yes

versus

Q: What did you think of last month's sales meeting?
A: I really enjoyed the presentation Bob made.

As you can see, you can get a more detailed answer from someone with an open-ended question. Other open-ended questions include the following:

Q: What other speakers did you enjoy?

Q: Why did you enjoy Bob's presentation?

Q: How do you think the team will do with the new goals in place?

The list can go on and on, and so will the conversation. Now for the C, compliment. Compliments can help break the ice, but the key is to give a compliment that doesn't come across as phony. Be sure to make the compliment early in the conversation, perhaps as an icebreaker.

- **Say:** Your necklace is stunning.
- **Don't say:** Your necklace is stunning. How much did it cost?

It's not appropriate to ask someone how much something costs or even where it's from, whether it's clothes, accessories, or jewelry, as it forces someone to essentially say how much something costs, which could make them uncomfortable. If you are asked how much something costs and it makes you uncomfortable to answer, you can deflect by telling an anecdote about the item or replying that you don't remember or that it was a gift. Don't compliment how an item, such as a dress, looks on the person. Stick to the item itself.

- **Say:** I like the color of your dress.
- **Don't say:** That dress looks great on you.

If you know the person, compliment something they've done at work or in a social setting. A compliment on an intangible accomplishment can come across as more authentic.

- **Say:** I really enjoyed the presentation you gave last week on (insert topic here).
- **Don't say:** You looked great when you gave that presentation last week.

Make New Friends

How do you forge these relationships? When meeting new people, find something you have in common with them, make a light joke, and show genuine interest in what they are talking about. Instead of focusing on business topics such as what the person does or what their business goals and plans are, you can ask a mixture of open and closed conversation starters:

- How or why they come to the event?
- How did they hear about the event?
- These (insert food items) are delicious. Have you tried them?
- This venue is beautiful. Have you been here before?
- Did you see the (team name) game last night?
- How do you know (name of someone you think you both know)?

You can also get creative and ask questions such as:
- I'm planning a trip for summer. Any fun West Coast destinations you think are a must-see?
- If you could have dinner with any historical figure, who would it be?

Being Likable

A simple trick to come across as more likable when talking to people is looking into their left eye. Looking into someone's left eye causes you to break posture as you lean in naturally. It shows that you're engaged in the conversation and listening to what the other person is saying. If you want to come across as more assertive, look into the person's right eye. Looking into someone's right eye causes you to square your shoulders, giving you the power posture discussed on page 121 with your chin parallel to the floor. This more formal stance gives nonverbal cues that you mean business. If you're wondering what to do if the person has a lazy eye or a medical condition, such as pink eye, look in their other eye as you would not want to draw attention to it or make them feel uncomfortable.

Who Are the People in Your Network?

If you think the only people worth networking with are those you work with at your company or in your industry, you'd be missing out on a diverse range of groups you may be able to connect with and benefit from. So, who are the people in your network?

School Friends

Don't limit your school chums to just the people you went to college with. High school, middle school, and even elementary school friends you've kept in touch with over the years on Facebook, Instagram, and LinkedIn may be able to connect you to and introduce you to members of their own business networks.

Relatives

You may be surprised at how many people your parents, grandparents, and other relations may know. Through their colleagues, neighbors, golf buddies, college friends, members of their house of worship, or other associations, they may be able to introduce you to senior-level (hiring) managers at companies you may want to work for or people you can pitch business to.

Colleagues

The people you work with, starting way back from high school summer jobs through college internships and into your present role, are all part of your network. Don't limit your colleagues only to people who worked on your team or at the same level. You have probably interacted with a wide range of employees at each job you've had from assistants to managers and even c-suite executives. Don't be afraid to maintain relationships with all of them personally and digitally on LinkedIn.

Almost Everyone You Interact With

Don't be surprised if your neighbor, doctor, or someone in your book (or any type of) club or group turns out to have a great connection or resource for you. While you don't want to quiz people on who they know before you decide to befriend them, don't be surprised if one day when mentioning that you're looking for a new job or a vendor to help on a project if they volunteer a contact for you to reach out to.

Not sure about some of these people being part of your network? My business partner, Anne, has a great story about why you should think more broadly when determining who should be in your network. While in college, Anne was visiting her grandmother, who had some friends over. One of them, Mrs. Bromley, had been Anne's piano teacher and was now over eighty years old. She asked Anne what she wanted to do when she graduated, and Anne told her that she wanted to work at a magazine. Well, Mrs. Bromley told Anne that one of her friends had a daughter who worked at the new *O, The Oprah Magazine* and that she would tell her about Anne and that Anne should look her up and call her. Anne wasn't so sure that Mrs. Bromley had such a great connection, but she promised her that she would reach out, so Anne picked up a copy of *O, The Oprah Magazine* and the first name on the masthead, under Oprah, was Mrs. Bromley's friend's daughter, the editor-in-chief! Anne picked up the phone and called Hearst Magazines and asked to speak to the editor-in-chief, who was expecting Anne's call, because Mrs. Bromley called and told her Anne would be calling. They had a lovely conversation about taking piano lessons at Mrs. Bromley's and she asked Anne to forward her résumé. There weren't any job openings at that time, but the point of the story is that Anne's grandma's friend's daughter was the editor-in-chief of a major magazine, and, because Anne opened her network to her grandmother's friends, she was able to get her résumé into the right hands!

Managing Bad Networkers

Even with the best intentions, sometimes the person you are talking to doesn't take the hint that the conversation has ended. It happens. They may tag along as you try to work the room. Or perhaps the person is a close talker and when they speak you can feel their breath on your face. Here are some tips to help you manage "the shadow networker" and "the close talker."

The Shadow Networker

The shadow networker is most likely unsure of whom to speak with or where to go, so once they find a friendly person, they may not want to part from them. Not sure what the signals are? If you've ended the conversation, or at least tried to, you may not be sending the right message. Don't say you're leaving them to:

- Get a drink, because a shadow networker may join you.
- Use the restroom, because a shadow networker may join you.

- Step outside for fresh air, because a shadow networker may join you.

To end a conversation, you need to be direct and say that you enjoyed meeting or speaking with them and that you look forward to speaking or seeing them in the future, and then walk away. Handing over or exchanging business cards is another way to close a conversation.

The Close Talker

Whether someone is angry or very into you, they may come too close and not be respectful of your personal space. If this happens, I will teach you the Meier Method technique called "The Tango," which subtly allows you to put physical space between yourself and someone else. You can use this technique to come across as though you are listening without allowing your body to appear as though you are startled.

Interestingly, I had a major airline company come to us to ask for help in dealing with customers in tense situations, and after teaching them this tactic, the group training director said it was one of the most-used techniques they as a team had ever learned. Here's how you do it:

Step 1: Plant one foot firmly on the floor.

Step 2: Place your other foot a step behind you and keep your feet a step-width apart, creating an invisible line on the floor that the other person won't cross, unless they want to tango.

Is Your Net Working for You?

Networking is all about relationships. To get the most out of your network, you have to do more than just cultivate new relationships, you have to nurture them. Here's how:

Foster a Relationship

Networking shouldn't be limited to a transactional relationship. Add meaning to the connection by sending birthday wishes (over email is fine) and holiday greetings (a card is more meaningful), and touching base throughout the year in a relevant way. If the person gets a promotion or is featured in a news story, send them your congratulations, or if you come across something you think would interest them, forward it to them.

Networking Is Not a Quid Pro Quo

In other words, do something to help someone because it's the right thing to do, not because you expect them to help you in return. This doesn't mean they won't return the favor one day, but if you expect or demand some action in return, you'll find that fewer people will seek you out and your network will dwindle.

Stay Relevant

Post regularly on social media, a blog, or website with content that people in your network may see. Maybe it's an industry-related article that you're reposting or something you wrote related to the field. Either way, you want people to think of you when they are seeking someone knowledgeable or connected in business.

Be Honest

While no one wants to deliberately hurt someone's feelings, it won't help anyone to offer up advice or a connection that you know won't be of any benefit or could actually harm them professionally. Instead of declining a request to make an introduction or pass along a résumé, tell the person why you don't think it's a good idea to move in that direction. He or she may be hurt at first, but at least they know they can always trust you to tell them the truth, and in the end that will actually strengthen your connection.

The Little Things Matter

Not every networking assist has to be a grand gesture. You can help someone by suggesting a great restaurant to take clients or the best hotel to stay at when in a certain city. These helpful suggestions, no matter how trivial they may seem, all add up to strengthening the connections you have made.

Say Thank You

If someone helps you by making an introduction for you or recommending you for a position, it's important to show them you appreciate the gesture. In addition to saying thank you, write a handwritten thank-you note, and if you got a new job or client from their recommendation, consider sending a gift. Some gifts people will appreciate are a basket of fruit, a box of baked goods, or a gift card.

Chapter 6

Dining

I can look across a table at a business dinner and see instantly who has been trained in formal dining etiquette just by the way they hold their cutlery or how they unfold their napkin into their lap. Practicing formal dining manners at a table tells everyone you are dining with that you respect them enough to be on your best behavior. The number of times a company has brought me and my team in to help all levels of employees from associates to c-suite level is endless. From casual dining to black-tie galas, if you are representing your company or hosting clients, knowing and practicing good dining etiquette is crucial.

Imagine taking potential new clients out to a lunch to try to convince them to work with you. You of course take them to a nice meal to show them how important they are, but with that comes a multicourse prix fixe meal. Your eyes widen when you see the servers scurry over to place all the pieces of silverware on the table that you will need to enjoy the meal. As they do this, you begin to panic. Which do you pick up first? What is that little knife for, and who orders the wine for all these courses? The table is finally set, and the first course is placed in front of you. The correct etiquette is that you, the host, should tell everyone to "please enjoy" as a signifier to begin the meal, but you didn't know that, so eventually everyone just begins. Then you can't focus on selling your services to your prospective clients because you are so insecure about which fork or knife to pick up next. This scenario is all too common, and with just a little training, is completely avoidable. Read on to learn how to master dining etiquette so that you can dine with confidence!

How to Hold Cutlery

One thing you can do in business to instantly make yourself look like a polished professional at the dining table is hold your cutlery correctly. In casual dining in America you can pick up your fork and knife, cut up to four pieces of food, rest your knife down on the plate, and then eat your food with your fork (prongs up) in your dominant hand. The moment you enter a formal dining situation in America, or always in business, I recommend you switch to what I call the "Continental style" of holding your silverware. No matter if you are left- or right-handed, in Continental style the fork always stays in the left hand and the knife in the right hand. The spoon is always held in the dominant hand. The Meier Method of holding your cutlery correctly in formal dining is called

American Dining

Continental Dining

the "Index, Wrap, and Twist" (IWT). Let's begin with the fork. Simply pick up the fork and put it in your open, flat palm. Hold it so it balances along your left index finger. Now, pick up the knife with your right hand and hold it so that the blade is facing upward and resting along your right index finger. Then, wrap all of the other fingers into the palm of your hand. Finally, flip your wrists around so that they are now facing the plate. You should have flat index fingers and also make sure that your index fingers are on the handle of each piece of cutlery and not on the bridge, prongs, or blade of the fork and knife. To hold a spoon correctly, first, simply place it in your dominant hand. Your index and thumb are on the top of the spoon and the other fingers are wrapped into your palm.

Index

Wrap

Twist

Do Our Hands Go above or under the Table When Not Eating?

In American and British dining, we keep our hands under the table at all times until we reach above the table to either eat, drink, or gesture. When dining in most other parts of the Western world (think Brazil to Germany), we would keep our wrists on the table at all times, from the moment we sat at the table.

Resting Cutlery

To pace yourself so that you finish eating at about the same time as your dining companion, you want to take a break after four bites of food to either clean your mouth with your napkin or perhaps have a sip of water. In the US, here is how you rest your cutlery to signify to the server that you are either still eating or that you are finished when dining in the United States:

Cutlery break

Cutlery finished

Holding Glassware

The main thing to remember is that if your glass has a stem, you should hold it by the stem. Why? We hold our glasses by the stem and not the bowl of the glass for two reasons. First, it can leave fingerprints all over beautiful glassware. The second and more important reason is because we can heat the liquid in the glass, which makes it deviate from the temperature at which it was meant to be served. By changing the temperature of wine, you are actually changing the flavor of

the wine. Many people hold white wine by the stem, but what about red wine? As many red wines are served at room temperature, is it okay to hold a red wine glass by the bowl? No! Even red wine should be held at the stem because we would never want to heat the wine to more than room temperature, and certainly not to body temperature of 98.6°F. To hold a glass with a stem, hold it with a minimum of your thumb, index, and middle fingers. The lower to the stem you hold, the more sophisticated a hold it becomes as your hand is farther removed from the liquid.

Beware of the "Lip Ring"

Have you ever been at a cocktail party and looked down at your glass to see a literal ring around the rim of the glass, either of unsightly lipstick or even natural oil from your skin or lip balm? To avoid this, drink from the same point of the glass the entire time. It takes a bit of consciousness to do, but once you master it, it will become a habit and you'll look much more polished at your next event.

Napkin Etiquette

When you walk into a restaurant, the moment you sit down in your chair you should take the napkin and put it on your lap. When you are at a dinner party at a private home, you should wait until the host or hostess puts the napkin in their lap before you follow suit. This is so we do not rush the host or hostess, who may look back at the table and

see his or her guests ready and hungry with napkins on their laps before everyone is seated. Never announce to the dining room in a restaurant that you are going to the restroom. Instead, say "Please excuse me." Then, pinch your napkin in the middle and place it in

your chair to signify to the server that you are coming back. At the end of the meal, pinch the napkin and put it on the table where your fork used to be.

Why We Say "Please Enjoy" and Not "Bon Appétit!"

The French phrase "bon appétit" means "good digestion," and some people might find it gross to talk about the physical digestion process. Somewhere down the line, these words made it across the pond and were mistaken for a "fancy" way to tell people to eat, when, as you now know, it is really quite the opposite!

Navigating a Place Setting

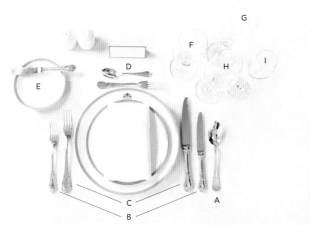

Example of a formal four-course American meal including (A) soup, (B) starter, (C) main course, (D) dessert, (E) bread, (F) water, (G) red wine, (H) white wine, (I) champagne

The fork is always to the left side of the dining plate (prongs facing up) in Western dining, and we can remember this because it has four prongs and the word "left" also has four letters. The knife is set on the right side of the plate. We can remember this because the word knife has five letters, and so does the word right. The spoon, also with five letters, is placed on the right. The bread plate always goes to the left of the dining plate and the drinks always go to the right. You can remember this by thinking of the acronym BMW, which stands for the order in which a table is set: **B**read, **M**eal, **W**ater/**W**ine. If you see silverware at the top of the plate, this is for dessert, and you can remember this because it's at the top of the plate and the farthest thing away from you and the last thing you'll reach for.

Navigating Multiple Courses

You've probably heard the general rule of thumb to start from the outside and work your way in. One thing I like to add to that is you typically start on the side that has more pieces of cutlery. So, if there

Three course meal: a starter, main, and dessert

is a fork on the left and a knife and spoon on the right side of the plate, you know you should pick up the spoon first. If the table is set with equal numbers on both sides, such as a main dining fork and knife and a starter fork and knife, then you know you should pick up both sides together.

Eating Politely

Every year my team and I fly all over the world training thousands of people in dining etiquette. We see the same common mistakes time and time again, so I thought it might be helpful to include some of the most frequently asked questions and faux pas while dining:

1. As the host, once everyone has their plate of food, you should say "Please enjoy" to signify to everyone that they should start eating. If you'd like to make a toast before you start eating, now is the time! If one of your guests does not have their meal, it's up to you to politely flag the server to check on their meal. You should always wait until everyone has their meal to begin eating. If your meal is the last to come out, you should verbally signal to everyone to begin by saying "Please everyone, begin while it's still warm," and they should then follow your lead and begin.

2. **We cut one piece of food at a time in business etiquette.**

3. **Dining is strategic in the way that you can mix two foods together at once.** For instance, if you have chicken, potatoes, and green beans on a plate you could put a piece of chicken on the fork as well as a piece of a potato. You would not, however, add a third food such as a green bean, as the fork starts to look too full and overloaded.

4. **When passing food around the table, pass going right around the table.**

5. **In the United States and United Kingdom, you want to leave a little bit of something on your plate to show your host that you are satisfied, but in the rest of the Western world, you typically want to finish everything on your plate to show your host that you are satisfied.**

6. **The rule with communal foods, such as a big pizza on the table to share, is you would not take anything straight from a shared plate and put it into your mouth.** Instead, you would take a piece of pizza from the communal pizza pie and put it on your own plate and then eat from that. Common communal foods include sandwiches, pizza, tapas, oysters, sushi, and French fries.

7. **At a cocktail party, if a server offers you a plate of small bite-sized hors d'oeuvres, make sure to take the napkin first, followed by the piece of food you want to eat.**

8. **It's very common in a work environment to have buffet-style eating.** If this is the case, it's up to you to get your own plate of food, silverware, napkin, and sometimes even drinks. Make sure not to

overfill your plate to avoid any piling or overflowing of food. Make sure to avoid foods with garlic or heavy flavors that may linger long after you're done with your meal.

9. Always use your right hand to pass things to others at the table. This is a custom that is cultural.

10. Lips stay sealed while chewing food. This sounds basic, but the number of well-educated and high-ranking people in business I see chewing with their mouths open or talking while eating is astonishing. If you have food in your mouth, your lips should stay zipped and you should breathe through your nose until you swallow your food. There should be no noise coming from your mouth while chewing or swallowing, or lip- or tongue-smacking as you eat.

11. Do not chew ice. Ever. That crunching sound is almost as bad as the sound of cracking your knuckles.

12. If you feel something in your teeth, try to remove it by closing your mouth and loosening it with your tongue. Do not use a toothpick or your finger. If you are unable to clear whatever it is in your teeth, excuse yourself to the restroom to do any and all grooming there.

Tip Time!

Should you tell someone if there is food in their teeth? Yes! The correct etiquette is to quietly tell the person there is something, whether it be lipstick or spinach, stuck on a tooth. If the tables were turned, you certainly would want to know so you could fix the issue, too!

Parts of the Plate You Should Know

There are two parts of a plate you should know to help you eat neatly. If a plate is the shape of a clock, with the top being 12:00, remember to always put things you are not eating such as garnishes, small fish bones, or lemon rinds in the "discard section" or 11:00 position. Sauces and butters go in the 5:00 position. You should always leave the rim of the plate clean as

Table setting for soup

a gesture of respect to service staff who may get their fingers dirty when they come to clear your plate.

Bread and Soup Etiquette

Soup is the only food in Western dining that we eat by scooping away from us. Never fill the bowl of the spoon all the way when scooping back. Never blow on your soup to cool it down as it could fly off the spoon onto the table. The correct way to cool it off is by stirring in the shape of a crescent moon at the top half of your soup bowl. The only two countries in which it is okay in formal etiquette to use bread to dunk or sop up soup or sauce are France and Italy. If you have a bread roll and you want to butter it, use your butter knife if you have one but remember to never cut the bread. Only use the butter knife to spread butter onto the bread. We only break bread rolls; we don't cut them. Only rip off the one piece of bread you are eating at a time. Keep the bread roll touching the bread plate as you tear off pieces and butter the bread so you don't create bread crumbs.

Coffee and Tea Etiquette

Holding a coffee cup is different from holding a teacup in formal etiquette. When holding a coffee cup or mug, we loop our index finger through the cup handle and put our thumb on the top of the handle. For a teacup, it's a bit different. We typically have less tea served in a cup than coffee, and oftentimes the cups are made of more delicate material such as fine or bone china. We hold the teacup by pinching our index finger with our thumb beneath the top of the cup's handle, and then lining our middle finger along the bottom of the handle to support it. Think "pinch and support." It may feel funny at first if you are not used to this method of holding, and if this method of holding, and if

Holding a coffee cup

Holding a teacup

that is the case, you can use your index and middle finger from your other hand to hold and support the cup from the other side.

Wine

If you are the host of the meal, it's up to you to order wine for the table. If you don't know a lot about wine, you may ask for recommendations from the restaurant's server, or if it's a formal restaurant, they are likely to have a sommelier. The important part is to ask what type of wine everyone would like before ordering a bottle for the table. If some people want red and some want white, you may want to get a bottle of each if budget allows. If everyone prefers to order single glasses of wine, then each person can order for themselves. If you are brave enough to pass off the menu to someone you are hosting to order bottles for the table, beware that they may order out of your budget and you'll still be responsible for the bill at the end of the meal.

Seating Precedence

If you are hosting clients or planning a seating chart, remember that the most important person in business goes to the host's right. If there are two hosts, you have two places to put VIPs. If there is one host and there are two VIPs, the host can put one person to their left and one person to their right. This way the host can always make sure their important guests are being taken care of and are having great conversation.

Communication with Service Staff

There is nothing worse than someone who is rude to service staff. Think back to the story I told you at the beginning of this book about the candidate who lost the position to someone else because of his interactions with the server (page 2). It's important to always show the utmost respect to anyone in the service industry, especially because they are helping us. People oddly think that because someone is being paid to help us, they can be treated differently, which couldn't be further from the truth. From the restaurant hostess to the server, manager, bartender, busser, chef, sommelier, and coatcheck person, these are all positions in hospitality that deserve kind, patient communication. Remember, these are all someone's mother, father, brother, sister, or friend, and you wouldn't want any of those people in your life to ever be treated badly. If you are calling a server over for the bill, avoid snapping, clapping, or aggressively waving toward them, as it's seen to many service personnel as condescending. Instead, simply raise two fingers together (middle and index fingers) slightly above your shoulder and make eye contact with the server and say "Check, please."

Tip Time!

In modern etiquette, we call waiters "servers" to take out the reference that they are simply there to wait on us.

Handbags and Briefcases

The connotation in the United States is that if your handbag is on the floor there is nothing of value in it. If your bag is large, like a briefcase, and you don't want to check it because of its contents, then it goes underneath the table by your top left toe, so it stays out of the way of service staff coming and going from the sides of the table. I advise thinking ahead before you choose a bag for a formal meal. Something small can fit behind your back or even under your napkin.

When Is It Okay to Take off a Suit Jacket or Blazer at a Dining Table?

Only remove it once the most senior or important person at the table has done so. For example, if you are sitting at an eight-person round table and your boss keeps their suit jacket on, you should, too. Remember in formal dining, you would keep your dinner jacket buttoned by the top button and then right before you sit down, unbutton it to give yourself space to sit. When you get up from the table again, you would button the top button again.

Tipping

Tipping is cultural. It is customary to tip in America as a gesture to show that you recognize or appreciate good service. If at a restaurant, you should tip 15 to 20 percent of the check at the end of the meal. You do not have to tip on the tax, just on the total cost of food and beverage. If the service was bad, you should still tip a minimum of 15 percent and never complain in front of clients. If after the meal when you are no longer with clients and feel you did not get the service you deserved, you can then call the restaurant and ask to speak to a manager.

It is not customary to tip at a takeout counter. If when at a takeout counter you think the service was great or the person helping you was exceptional, then it's absolutely a very nice thing to tip if you wish. That being said, it should never be expected at a counter that you will tip. For instance, if you buy a coffee at a takeout counter and you barely spoke to the person taking your order, you shouldn't feel pressure to tip. If someone went above and beyond in any way when taking your order, then you are welcome to leave one.

If you are hosting clients, I always advise to bring single dollar bills with you to restaurants in case you ever need to tip the coat-check person. It's typically one to two dollars per coat, and if you are taking care of clients, you would pay for theirs, too.

Doggie Bags

No doggie bags in business. This means that whenever you are at a nice restaurant hosting clients or with your team at a professional meal, it's not appropriate to ask for a doggie bag—no matter how delicious that steak was!

Chapter 7

Interviews, Résumés & Thank-You Notes

You will be going on interviews, in one form or another, through-out your career. Applying for a new position at another company is one type of interview, but you may also have to interview for a new position or promotion within your current company, and potential clients will interview you when deciding if they want to hire you and your company. Interviewing is all about confidence. This can be shown in both verbal and nonverbal ways, through your résumé, your appearance, your timeliness or tardiness, and how you conduct yourself during the interview process. You may have heard the phrase "Dress for the job you want, not the one you have." Keep this in mind when you go on interviews to help you get into the mind-set of already having the position or the client. Here are some more things to keep in mind while going on interviews.

Asking for a Job Interview

When sending your résumé or applying for a job, use your cover letter or email to express interest. Don't be demanding about it, but make it clear that you would like to speak with them either over the phone or in person, and can make yourself available. A phone interview may be able to happen sooner as it can take less time. This is a good way to get your foot in the door, so if one is offered, take it. Make sure your cell service is good, or use a land-line, and that you are in a quiet space.

Include any of these phrases in your cover letter to request an interview:

- I look forward to speaking with you about the position.
- I look forward to learning more about the position.
- I am available to meet with you.
- I look forward to connecting with you soon.
- I can be reached at this email address (insert email here) or over the phone at 941-555-0173.

If you want to reach out by phone and don't know the name of the hiring manager, call the main number and ask to speak to someone in the human resources department. Once you're transferred, intro-duce yourself and explain that you sent your résumé in regard to (insert position here) and that you're calling because you would like to schedule an interview. Be very polite and understanding if you're told that they are not setting up interviews yet or if they haven't reviewed your résumé. And note that if the job posting states that you should not call, don't call. Do not show up unannounced or uninvited to a company's office asking to meet with the hiring man-ager or a human resources representative.

How to Behave on an Interview

It's extremely important that you put your best foot forward and come prepared to answer questions about yourself as well as have questions to ask the person interviewing you. Learn as much as you can about the company's culture to know what you should wear. Jeans and sneakers may be appropriate for a job at a casual tech start-up, but if you're applying for a finance or legal position, it's probably a good idea to wear a dark-colored suit. Regardless of the fact that the hiring manager and human resources representative already have your résumé, you should bring several copies with you in case they didn't print out a copy for the interview. And be enthusiastic about the opportunity. Don't be afraid to say why you want to work at the company and what excites you about the position.

Make Your Résumé Relevant

Your résumé will tell a potential employer a lot about you—what your experience is, what your skills are, where you went to school, etc., so it's very important that it is easy to read and organized. Do not exaggerate or outright lie on your résumé as many of the details will be fact-checked by a potential new employer. Résumés should be limited to one page. When you reach the management and c-suite level, your résumé can grow to a second page, but focus on the highlights of the positions you've had—main responsibilities and accomplishments—as well as what would be relevant to this hiring manager and company. Here are some helpful tips:

- **For the header, have your name with your phone number and email address listed beneath it.** Do not waste space with your mailing address.
- **Choose a font that is easy to read and at a size that one does not need a magnifying glass to read.**
- **Including an objective is debatable.** Objectives tend to take up a number of lines that may be better used for your accomplishments.
- **Organize your résumé into several sections: Education, Experience, and Skills.**

- **List all relevant experience.** If you're applying for a sales position at a technology company and you're several years post college, remove your pre-college job experience. Focus on past internships, past positions, and your current position. As your career advances you can remove the earliest positions such as internships.

- **Education should include the college(s) you graduated from, the degree(s) you have received, and any honors.** You can also include certificate programs that are relevant.

- **Include the names of specific skills that are applicable to the role you're applying for.** Skills can vary from computer programs to languages.

- **Activities and interests are similar to objectives in that they can take up space and not everyone finds them necessary.** If you do choose to include some of yours, list charities and organizations you're involved with as well as other activities you participate in.

Informational Interviews Matter

An informational interview is a great opportunity to meet with a company's human resources representative or senior-level employee to learn more about a company or industry. An informational interview is specifically about getting information and not necessarily a position. Both you and the person you're meeting with know a job offer is not part of the conversation, but it is a great opportunity for a company to become familiar with you and for you to help determine if this is an industry or career you're interested in pursuing.

Just because a job offer is not in the cards doesn't mean you shouldn't come prepared for the meeting. Have a list of questions with you about the position, bring a copy of your résumé, to give only if it's asked for, and dress appropriately. Don't forget to bring a notebook and pen to take notes. The person you're meeting with may be able to recommend someone else you should reach out to as well as websites, newsletters, and professional organizations you may want to follow or join. And keep in mind that an informational interview could lead to a job opportunity down the road. Now that the company is aware of you, your background, and interest, they may reach out to you if there's an open position that you're qualified for.

> ## Tip Time!
>
> Look to your network to find people you may want to have an informational interview with. A friend, relative, or first connection on LinkedIn may be able to open a door for you to someone or a company that you're interested in learning more about.

Following up after Applying for a Job

You may not get an immediate reply after you've emailed your résumé or applied through a company's website, so following up is a great way to touch base with the human resources or hiring manager. You can send a follow-up email or call their office to confirm that they received your résumé, and possibly get an interview date on the calendar. Don't follow up within a few days; wait at least a week or two before reaching out. Some people are more comfortable sending and receiving emails than they are using the phone. If you're one of them, write a concise and courteous email to confirm that they have your résumé on file, and ask for an interview. This email is not a cover letter and should get straight to the point. See an example of a thank-you email on the next page.

Dear (name of the person you sent your résumé to),

I hope you had a lovely weekend. I am writing to follow up on my application for (name of position). I submitted my résumé several weeks ago and am very interested in working at (name of company).

I can be reached at this email address or over the phone at 312-555-0143, and am available to meet with you or schedule a phone interview regarding the position.

I look forward to hearing from you, and thank you for your consideration.

Best regards,

(Your name)

Job Interview Tips to Keep in Mind

There are a number of ways to put your best foot forward when on a job interview. Researching the company, bringing a list of questions with you to ask, and familiarizing yourself with the job description are all important to show your enthusiasm and interest in the role. Here are my top ten tips to keep in mind when preparing for a job interview.

1. Rehearse the answers to common interview questions. You know you will be asked about your work experience, projects you were involved with, and your strengths and weaknesses.

2. Be ready to share examples of your work.

3. When answering questions, be concise and tie them back to your skills and relevant work experience.

4. Draft a list of professional references. Before handing this list to a potential employer, confirm with the people you're listing that they are comfortable being a reference for you, and tell them what company and position you're applying for.

5. Select what you will wear to the interview the night before so that you're not rushed in the morning. Make sure to pack a few copies of your résumé, as well as a notebook and a pen, too.

6. Arrive five to ten minutes prior to your appointment to ensure that you have time to get acclimated to the setting. If you're not sure where the building is located, you can do a test drive or public transportation test a few days before.

7. Remember to be polite to everyone you meet at the company from the receptionist to the hiring manager.

8. Practice positive body language. Have good posture and avoid crossing your arms when speaking with people because it gives the impression that you don't want to be there.

9. Don't speak negatively about previous employers and colleagues.

10. Ask about next steps. Are there other people they want you to meet with? Is there a test? Do they want to see more examples of your past work?

Thank-You Notes Can Make a Difference

After someone has taken the time to meet with you, whether it's an informational or job interview, it's important to send a thank-you note that is handwritten. The three or four lines can reference something that was said during the interview as well as your appreciation for the time or excitement for the role and next steps. Make sure your handwriting is legible so the person can easily read your note. To ensure the people you are writing to receive it quickly, bring a stamped and addressed envelope with you and after you've left the building, write the note and drop it in a nearby mailbox or local post office to ensure it arrives within a few days.

So, what should you write in your thank-you note? Believe it or not, don't start with the words "Thank you." Instead, start with another phrase such as "I appreciate" or "I enjoyed" because it is unexpected and the person is likely to pay more attention to what you've written. You can include the phrase "Thank you" after your initial first or second line, and then mention something that stuck with you about your interaction. Before signing off with "Best regards," add a line about connecting, speaking with, or hearing from them soon. Below are some examples of handwritten thank-you notes.

For a Position at a New Company

Dear (interviewer's name),

I enjoyed meeting with you today for the (job title) position. Thank you for the opportunity to learn about the role and (company name).

(Mention something specifically discussed such as a company goal, or how your experience aligns with the position).

I look forward to hearing from you regarding next steps.

Best regards,

(Your name)

For an Informational Interview

Dear (name of person you met with),

I appreciate you taking the time to meet with me. I learned so much more about the (name of industry) and look forward to a future career in it!

I will check out the (website, blog, newsletter, etc.) that you recommended, and keep you informed of my next steps as I grow in the field.

Best regards,

(Your name)

For a Potential New Client

Dear (client's name)

It was a pleasure meeting with you earlier today. I enjoyed learning more about (company name) and your goals for the coming year.

Based on our conversation (note the key points and how they align with your company's offerings).

I'd be delighted to schedule a follow-up call to review what our company offers and how we can help you reach your goals. Please let me know what your availability is in the next week and we can schedule a time on the calendar.

I look forward to working with you and your colleagues.

Best regards,

(Your name)

A Note on Stationery

It's important to purchase fine stationery that looks elegant and feels lovely, too. You have the option to choose boxed stationery cards that are a solid color, or feature your initial, name, monogram, or the words "Thank you." You can also customize a set of cards from a local stationer or online retailer. Here are some examples of the different styles of business stationery you can shop for:

- For brief notes, including thank-you notes after an interview, you can send a correspondence card, which is also called a flat card, or a fold-over card. Both styles are available in several dimensions, the most popular being A2 (4¼" x 5½"), A6 (4½" x 6¼"), and A7 (5" x 7").

- Monarch sheets, also known as "executive stationery" can have a letterhead printed or engraved at the top and are used for handwritten notes or printed letters. They are 7¼" x 10½" in size. A watermark by a high-end stationer may subtly appear on the sheet.

- Don't be afraid to choose stationery in a color other than stark white. Color can make a bold statement as well as stand out in a sea of white or cream-colored paper.

- When writing your note, you may want to type or make a handwritten draft of what you want to write to avoid making a mistake that you can't erase and should not cross out.

- Choose a good pen in black or blue ink to write your note.

- Only write your note on the front of the card or sheet of paper. If a correspondence or fold-over card doesn't give you all the space that you need, select a bigger size.

Chapter 8

Negotiations

A negotiation is not something to fear. It's a conversation, not a confrontation. Before you go into a negotiation for a salary at a new job, promotion, or raise, think about what you want to say and practice saying it so that your message is clear and understood.

Where to Begin

First, know what you're worth. Research what the going rate is for your position in your industry and in your city. Payscale.com and Glassdoor.com can be great resources when doing your research. You can also ask others in your field if you feel comfortable doing so. Another resource is job recruiters. When you're approached by one, ask them detailed questions about a position's responsibilities and salary. If they can't give you a target number, ask for a range. (We'll get to ranges later on.) Once you've done your homework, come up with a number or a range you feel comfortable asking for. If you don't have a number in mind, you are giving all the negotiating power to highly experienced negotiators like the human resources manager.

Preparing for the Conversation

Make notes to help you organize your thoughts. For a new job, think about your bargaining power or what you are bringing to the table:

- Education
- Training
- Years of experience
- Special skills

For a promotion and/or raise:

- Your accomplishments, including goals reached/surpassed
- Leadership at the company
- Tenure at the company
- Relationships with clients
- Another offer

Review your reasons and practice saying them. You can also ask someone to rehearse with you so you feel more comfortable and confident stating your reasons. Practicing ensures that you don't forget your points and that you can clearly communicate them. For a promotion or raise, you can also summarize your accomplishments on a single page or presentation to further show the goals you've reached and other accomplishments to make your point.

Go for the Higher End of the Range

It's safe to assume your employer or a potential employer will negotiate down from the number you offer. Therefore, ask for the higher end of the range so if they come back a little lower the number is still above the lower end of the scale for the position. Some negotiating experts will suggest that you avoid offering a range when making an offer because the employer will opt for the lower end of the range. Do what you feel comfortable asking for but have a range in mind in case you are asked for a salary range—and always ask for the higher end of the industry rate.

When to Ask for a Raise

Many people wait till their annual performance review to ask for a raise or promotion, but by then budgets may be set for the coming year. Instead, start bringing up the topic several months before when the company is still in planning stages for the next year. You also want to pick the right time to schedule the meeting. If you know the company is in the middle of a large project, help them complete it instead of asking for a raise in the middle of it. By waiting until the project is complete, you can then add it to your list of accomplishments and goals achieved. According to *Psychology Today*, you should ask for a raise or promotion on a Thursday or Friday when people are "most open to negotiation and compromise because we want to finish our work before the week is out."

Power Posture

Before you walk into a negotiation, stand tall with your chin parallel to the floor and shoulders squared to look and feel confident. Have a smile on your face so that you come across as friendly and positive. If you walk in with a scowl, you'll begin the meeting with a negative tone, and that isn't going to help your case. Once you're seated, maintain good posture. Remember, avoid using armrests or leaning back in the chair, as both break posture. Don't cross your arms in front of you, either, because it's a negative nonverbal cue that you're upset or angry.

Start Talking

Before requesting your starting salary at a new job, ask questions as to the specifics of the role and responsibilities as well as the department and company's priorities—are they looking for cost savings, are they expanding? Get a better understanding of what they are looking for before throwing out numbers. When negotiating a raise, keep a smile on your face and offer up some positive things to say about the company and team. Tell your manager that you enjoy working at the company and you want to expand on what you do. Then mention that you want to discuss a promotion and/or raise. Before you start talking numbers, start talking about your accomplishments. Take out your notes and explain/show your manager what you have achieved in the last quarter, year, throughout your tenure. And share the highlights of your tenure with the company, when you went above and beyond your role. State your case. Then, talk about your next steps at the company. What goals do you have set up to accomplish in the coming months or year? What can you do to lighten the workload of your manager? What new initiatives and ideas can you take charge of? What you don't want to address are your personal expenses—your rent has gone up or you want to buy a new car—as you're not the only employee who has bills to pay. You'll get further with your negotiation if you stick to the position and why your performance warrants a higher salary or raise.

The Numbers

If you are the one who called the meeting to ask for a raise, you should put a number on the table first. By putting your number on the table first, the rest of the negotiation will be based on that number. Ask for more than you want, so you can be an active bargaining partner and the other side of the table feels like they can get a deal, too. Remember that some companies may offer additional vacation days, allow you to work from home, a company car, and other incentives if they can't meet the dollar amount that you're asking for. Decide for yourself what those added incentives are worth, because working from home a few days a week and having an extra two weeks paid vacation could be worth agreeing to a lower salary amount.

Listening Is Just as Important as Stating Your Case

Remember to listen to what the other person is saying. If they are giving you reasons why a raise at this time is not possible, such as financial issues at the company or that they have already determined the budget for the next year, don't persist on a raise. Think on your feet with what else you want out of the conversation. Maybe it's a discussion in a month or three to revisit the topic, or maybe you want a title change now with a promise of a raise or bonus on a certain date. Don't ignore what the other person is saying as you need information to further the negotiation in your favor. To let the person know you're listening, you can nod your head slightly to give them a nonverbal cue. And if you hear something that you're confused about, it's okay to ask questions.

Countering with Kindness

If the company has come back to you with a lower number than you asked for or want to accept, be very cordial in your reply and express that you would like to work with them or that you enjoy working with them, but you were hoping that based on your work experience or work performance you could have a salary of (state the number you want here). Raising your voice and making threats will not help your argument and may actually cost you your job.

Negotiating over Email

Negotiations are most often done in person or over the phone, but if the hiring manger or recruiter prefers to keep your conversations over email, keep the messages friendly. Think about what you would say in person and fill your emails with pleasantries and courtesy. Remember that tone is sometimes hard to decipher in an email so read your email draft aloud before you press send to make sure that you're coming across in a friendly manner and not a hostile one.

"No" May Not Be Their Final Offer

Don't be afraid if you are told "no." Ask questions about what they are saying "no" to. Is it the number or the idea of a raise? Try to learn what they are thinking. What is the budget for the position? What would they be willing to offer in addition to or instead of a higher salary, perhaps a bonus tied to goals reached? What can you do to help them agree to your number? Can you add another responsibility to the role?

Chapter 9

Business Travel

You may be psyched to head off to a tropical locale or favorite city for an upcoming business trip, but don't forget that the keyword is "business," not "trip." A business trip means you are on company time from the moment you leave your home until you return, and representing the company, even when you're on "down time." Before you start planning a second itinerary filled with beach time, drinks, and other nonbusiness activities, keep the following points in mind to ensure that this trip isn't your last.

Be Prepared

The company is most likely sending you out of town to achieve one of several goals. It may be a sales meeting, industry conference, or other opportunity for you to put the company's best foot forward, and the best way to do that is to be prepared.

- **Make sure you have all the details for any meetings and appointments in your calendar.**
- **Have your travel itinerary including flight, hotel, and car rental details in an easy-to-find location.**
- **Know the names, titles, and roles of the people you will be meeting with so you don't mistake a senior-level person for an assistant.**

- **Have all the files and presentations you will need to present copyedited and organized so that you can easily access them.** And put an extra copy on a thumb drive so you have a backup in case your computer doesn't work.
- **Be on time for all meetings and appointments.** Map out in advance how long it will take you to get to each location and give yourself enough time to get from place to place. If you're running late, for whatever reason, let the people you are meeting with know.
- **Remember to bring business cards with you, and don't be afraid to bring extra in case you meet more people than planned.**

Traveling Internationally

If you're going to a foreign country, research the customs and etiquette for greeting people. You may also want to learn a few phrases such as "Hello" and "Goodbye," "Please" and "Thank you," "Nice to meet you," and "Where is the restroom?" Learn the exchange rate and have some of the local currency on you when you arrive. Ensure that your passport and any required visas or immunizations are organized and taken care of so there won't be any delays in entering the country. If you are concerned about meals due to a food allergy or dietary restriction, pack nonperishable items in your luggage. And remember to pack adapters so you can charge your phone, computer, and other gadgets.

This Is a Business Trip, Not an All-Expenses-Paid Vacation

On a vacation you may spend ample amounts of time by the pool, enjoy more than a few alcoholic drinks, and chat with friends and family about all sorts of things, but on a business trip you must not let professional boundaries fall by the wayside. Think of a business trip as time spent at the office, even if you're not in an office, and stick to these professional guidelines:

- **Don't gossip about colleagues, supervisors, or support staff members who aren't with you.**
- **While it's okay to have an alcoholic drink or two at a meal or cocktail party, don't overindulge to the point that you are drunk**. You don't want to do or say something that you will regret later.
- **Don't overshare.** These are your colleagues and/or clients, not your friends. Do not share stories about your personal life that may make someone feel uncomfortable.
- **Don't ask personal questions.** For the same reason you shouldn't overshare about your own life, avoid asking personal questions about the lives of your colleagues and clients. Stay away from questions about people's personal relationships with their spouses, families, health, etc.

Managing Travel Expenses

Before booking a business trip, a manager will approve the budget for the flight, hotel, and other expenses such as meals, cabs, and incidentals. A per diem (Latin for per day) will be allotted for meals based on the budget and average costs of meals in the city you're going to. (Some cities, such as New York City, may have a larger per diem because meals in that area are more expensive than in other parts of the country.) It's important to work with the company's travel agent, if there is one, to ensure that you're within budget when booking tickets and making reservations. Ask a manager or someone on the travel-planning team for hotel recommendations. The company may book exclusively with a specific hotel chain to ensure the best rate for business trips.

Stick to the budget the company sets for meals and keep all of your receipts. Write a quick note on each one noting if anyone else ate with you and what the final bill was after gratuity was added to it. Do this regardless of whether you paid cash, used a company credit card, or your own personal card. You may have to hand in all receipts in order to be reimbursed. The company may ask for an expense sheet to be handed in after the trip. Be sure to have all dates, total amounts, and reasons for each expense entered onto it and submitted soon after you return to the office. You won't be prevented from spending your own money on souvenirs, hotel amenities (such as a massage at the spa), or other nonwork essentials, but be sure that you don't submit receipts for reimbursements for these nonbusiness items. Below is a chart to help you figure out work and nonwork expenses on a business trip:

APPROVED BUSINESS TRIP EXPENSES	NOT-APPROVED BUSINESS TRIP EXPENSES
Airline, train, or bus tickets	Souvenirs and gifts
Car rental, including gas, insurance, and fees	Clothing, unless uniform related
Hotel, motel accommodations	In-room movie rentals
Meals (breakfast, lunch, and dinner)	Spa and fitness services
Snacks between meals	Costs for personal guest (If you have a friend join you for dinner, you can't expense their meal.)

APPROVED BUSINESS TRIP EXPENSES	NOT-APPROVED BUSINESS TRIP EXPENSES
Cab/taxi/Uber charges to and from business-related locations (i.e. airport to hotel, hotel to meeting)	Nonwork activities that charge a fee, such as admission to a museum, amusement park, etc.
Printing copies for meeting presentations	Alcohol consumed outside of a work setting

Be sure to check with your company to confirm which expenses are reimbursable on a business trip, as every company will have their own guidelines and per diems.

What to Wear and What Not to Wear

It's important to bring the proper attire for each occasion of your trip. Follow your company's dress code for official meetings and appointments with colleagues and clients. If the company expects male employees to wear a jacket and tie at the office, pack a jacket and tie for the trip. If open-toed shoes are not approved footwear at the office, it won't be when meeting with clients out of town either. Be sure your suitcase is professional and on brand for your company as well.

On Travel Days

When you'll be on a plane, train, or in a car for hours, it's okay to dress in business casual attire. You never know who you may run into at the terminal or on the plane or train, so it's important to avoid athleisure wear or pajamas, no matter how long your trip will be. Men and women can wear jeans, without rips, and women can wear flats. If you are heading straight from the airport or train station to a meeting, ensure that your work clothes are easy to grab when you open your carry-on bag or suitcase, and change in an airport restroom. For the return trip, if you're not leaving from the hotel but a meeting, change into your flight look upon your arrival at the terminal.

On Work Days

When packing for business meetings and events out of town, in addition to following the company's dress code, make sure your clothes are not wrinkled and look professional in all settings. Keep the climate of the area in mind. While it may be appropriate to wear a wool suit in Chicago in February, for a meeting in Florida, you can pick a lighter fabric. No matter the gender, style guidelines are similar in that all clothes should be tailored. Shoulders should be covered either by a shirt with sleeves or a jacket/blazer or cardigan. Avoid sleeveless shirts, tank tops, and camisoles unless they are worn under another layer. In a casual work setting, some companies may approve of designer but not athletic sneakers and open-toed sandals, but only if there is ankle support or a closed back. Double-check with your human resources department to confirm company policy before packing.

If you will be attending a social event such as drinks after work, a cocktail party, or gala, use the chart in chapter 1 (page 29) to help you determine the appropriate attire. Regardless of the occasion, err on the side of modesty when dressing and choose hemlines that are slightly above the knee or below. Strapless dresses are acceptable for cocktail and formal attire, but be sure to pack a wrap in case it's chilly outdoors or the air-conditioning is a bit strong.

On Downtime

After your work for the day is done and you want to relax by the pool or stroll around town and grab a bite, you shouldn't forget that you're still on a business trip. You can dress down in casual attire, but remember that you could bump into a client or colleague, so avoid athleisure, unless you're going for a run or to the hotel gym. Of course, a bathing suit is most appropriate for the pool, but pack a coverup for eating at the pool bar.

Chapter 10

Holiday Parties and Other Occasions

We all know that we spend more time with our coworkers than our families, so it's not uncommon for colleagues to celebrate happy occasions together whether they be birthdays, babies, and the holidays. For each of these parties there are set rules of etiquette that one should follow in order to show respect to each other, but also to not embarrass oneself. The most important thing to remember is that these are work events, even if they're held off-site at a restaurant or bar. The one exception would be a colleague's wedding, but we'll discuss that later on. Keeping in mind that these social occasions are still business events can help guide you in what you should wear, how to behave, and how much you should drink. Below you will find guidelines to help guide you through holiday parties and other celebrations.

Appropriate Behavior at Office Parties

It's important to remember that your manager, company executives, and members of the Human Resources team will most likely be attending an office party with you and your colleagues. Regardless of where the celebration is being held, it's not appropriate to say or behave in a manner that could embarrass you or the company. It's essential that you put your best business foot forward in the following ways:

- **If you're assigned any pre-party responsibilities, don't forget to fulfill them.** This includes bringing food or drinks to a potluck, chipping in for a group gift such as for a wedding or baby shower, or arriving early to help decorate.
- **Show up as close to the start time as possible.** Never be the last one to leave your holiday party!
- **Stick with the dress code or business attire.** Some party invitations will come with attire suggestions, such as "ugly holiday sweater" or "cocktail chic." (More on attire on page 29.)
- **If alcohol is available, whether at an open or cash bar, know your limit.** You don't want to wake up the next day not remembering how you got home, or worse, to an email of you doing something foolish or embarrassing, or be told that you've been fired.

What to Wear

When thinking about attire for an office party, if it will be held during the workday at the office, such as a colleague's wedding shower or baby shower, then whatever you wear to work regularly will be fine. The same goes for a meetup after work where you head over from the office. If it's a special event, such as the annual holiday party or summer picnic, or someone is being honored and it feels like more than drinks at the local bar, you may want to dress up a bit more for the occasion. Turn to page 29 for style and grooming tips for various business settings.

Party in the Conference Room

The most common types of office celebrations are birthdays, wedding showers, baby showers, and goodbye parties when someone is moving to another office location or leaving the company. If you're hosting one of these events, keep the following party-planning eti-quette in mind:

- **Invitations can be sent over email as a message and/or calendar invite.**
- **Remember to reserve the conference room in advance of the day.**
- **Let people know if they should bring their lunch or if snacks will be served.** Oftentimes these parties are held toward the end of the day when cake, cupcakes, and other pastries are served.
- **Decorations are not a must, but are a nice touch, especially for a wedding or baby shower.**
- **Let guests know if everyone should chip in on a wedding gift or baby gift, or if no gifts are necessary.**
- **Be aware of food allergies and dietary restrictions of those invited and ensure that there is something for everyone to enjoy.**

If a colleague is getting married, regardless of whether anyone at the office is invited to the wedding, it is a nice gesture to host a small wedding shower at the office. And the guest of honor should not feel pressured to invite colleagues who host a wedding shower at the office to the wedding.

Drinking While Working

Everyone should have a good idea of how many glasses of wine, champagne, beer, cocktails, etc. it will take for them to have reached their limit. Never hit your limit at an office party. It's important that you maintain your composure and self-control in the chance you find yourself next to the CEO at the buffet line or your boss on the dance floor. If you see a colleague who may be drunk, offer them a glass of water, a place to sit down, and possibly a ride home by either sharing a cab with them or calling a car to take them home. For those who do not drink alcohol, for whatever reason, don't feel obligated to. There should be plenty of nonalcoholic beverages available for you to choose from. But if you want to stop people from asking you why you're not drinking, try ordering a club soda with a lime, which usually does the trick.

Present and Accounted For

Gift giving at the office can vary depending on the occasion such as birthdays, weddings, babies, retirement, and holidays. Each department or team will have their own "rules" as to what occasions are appropriate to give a gift to a colleague. Below are things to keep in mind as well as answers to commonly asked questions about gifts at the office.

Around the Holidays

Secret Santa or white elephant parties are a great way to ensure that everyone receives a holiday present and can keep gifts within a specific price range. For secret Santa, make sure that everyone has been given someone to shop for and make clear what the budget range is. Twenty-five dollars is more than enough money to find a gift for someone. White elephant parties can also have a budget on the cost of gifts, and a white elephant gift exchange ensures that there are enough people buying items so that everyone walks away with something. Avoid giving clothing items that require a size because you could offend someone if you purchase the wrong one. And always show gratitude to the person who gave you the gift, regardless of what you received.

Holiday Gift Ideas for the Office by Category

- Food: Artisanal honey or jams, baked goods, candy, chocolate, dried fruit
- Lifestyle: Candles, games, journals, lotions, lunch carrier, mug, or festive glassware
- Technology: Charger, cord wrangler, headphones, wireless speaker
- Travel: Luggage tags, packing cubes, passport holder, reusable water bottle or hot cup, toiletry bag, travel wallet

Colleagues who are close to one another may decide to buy each other holiday gifts, and that's fine. You can exchange them away from others so no one feels left out. A great group gift idea is to bring a package of baked goods for the whole team to enjoy. Send a note around letting everyone know what was brought in so they can stop by the kitchen or your desk to enjoy the treats and say thank you as well as "Happy Holidays!" Managers may give a gift to subordinates, and assistants may receive a gift from their immediate supervisor. Depending on the relationship and the gift, one should send a thank-you note showing gratitude and appreciation. Be sure to mention the item in the note. See an example of a handwritten thank-you note on the next page. Be aware that your colleagues and clients may celebrate different holidays than you do, so "Happy Holidays" is a nice way to make sure everyone is included.

Dear Sam,

You know my taste so well! I absolutely love the monogrammed pencils. Thank you so much. As you can see, I'm already making great use of them.

I wish you and your family all the best this holiday season, and look forward to an exciting new year!

Best wishes,
Jennette

Weddings and Baby Showers

Regardless of whether office mates are invited to someone's wedding, an office wedding shower or group wedding gift is always a nice way to share in the celebration. Colleagues should look at the couple's wedding registry for gift ideas or come up with a present they think the couple will enjoy. The bride or groom should not feel obligated to invite colleagues because they host a shower or send a gift. A baby shower is also a wonderful way to show excitement! Similar to a wedding gift, shop the baby registry the expectant parents have created to find something they can use.

Birthdays, Retirement, and Other Reasons to Celebrate

There are a variety of other reasons to give a gift, including birthdays, someone leaving the company, or just for fun! There should never be an obligation to buy a gift for someone, but if it's customary at the office for everyone to chip in for various occasions, it's a good idea to participate as part of the team.

Tip Time!

Remember anything you say or do at an office holiday party or off-site *can* be used against you! What this means is essentially even though it is outside office hours, you are technically still at a work event and your actions or words can get you in trouble back in the office on Monday morning! Remain professional at all times, no matter the conversation, what you drink, or what you wear.

Final Thoughts

There's a lot of information to digest in this book, and it's meant to be kept as a resource to help you navigate your career path. You can turn to it when you decide to apply for a new job or in the days ahead of an interview. Flip to the networking section before going to a company event or industry conference, and the holiday party section if you're asked to participate in a white elephant party.

While there are hundreds of tips in this book to help you in your career, I wanted to share my personal top ten with you to always keep in mind in any business setting:

1. The most important tip to remember is that etiquette is about being courteous and kind and respectful to the people around you, whether they are your colleagues, support staff, executives, or clients. It doesn't cost anything to be nice to other people and it can pay you dividends in the end.

2. Always make a great first impression by entering a room using the 7-in-7 Theory, which includes:

- Physically enter a room with confidence and authority
- Be aware of your facial expression
- Ensure that your personal presentation is "on brand"
- Have a powerful and poised posture
- Use a confident and assertive voice
- Maintain positive body language and focused eye contact
- Evoke positive emotion in other people through our Charm Formula

3. When drafting an email, list the addresses in order of seniority and rank of positions. Start your message with "Dear" and sign off with "Best regards."

4. Don't forget to pack business cards every day, as you never know where you'll meet your next big opportunity. Always accept a business card in the manner it was offered to you, i.e., with one hand or two. And remember to look at both sides of the card before putting it in your pocket or bag.

5. In formal social occasions or any time in business settings, practice the Continental style of holding your cutlery, as shown on page 94. It's a sign to your dining companions that you have the utmost respect for them.

6. Don't be afraid to use the telephone. Sometimes a personal connection over the phone can help strengthen a relationship and close a deal.

7. When wearing a name tag to a business networking event, be sure to place it on the upper left side of your chest. In doing so, you won't block someone's view of it when you shake their hand.

8. Write a handwritten thank-you note to show your appreciation, as a tangible thank you is not commonly sent today and will be greatly valued. Here are several reasons to send a handwritten note:

- You are meeting with a human resources or hiring manager for a new job
- You want to show gratitude to a client

- Someone sends you a thoughtful gift for your birthday, engagement/wedding, or pregnancy

Bonus! Never start a thank-you note, whether over email or hand-written, with the words "thank you." Now that you've read this book, you know why! (Hint, page 116)

9. Remember that when you want to come across as likable, you look into the other person's left eye.

10. When negotiating a promotion, raise, or salary, it's important to prepare your case and be able to explain your accomplishments, experience, and other reasons you deserve that promotion, raise, or higher starting salary. Learn to pitch yourself.

About the Author

If you can be nothing else, be kind.
—Myka Meier

Entrepreneur and business etiquette coach Myka Meier founded Beaumont Etiquette to bring a fresh perspective to modern manners.

Co-founder of The Plaza Hotel Finishing Program and author of *Modern Etiquette Made Easy*, Myka travels the country as a keynote speaker and trainer to companies and employees, teaching what it takes to be the best in their industries.

A dual American and British citizen, Myka graduated with a degree in communications and trained at some of the world's most prestigious finishing schools. She was named "America's Queen of Good Manners" by *The Times* magazine, and has been featured across global media including *The Today Show*, *The New York Times*, *The Wall Street Journal*, *Good Morning America*, *TIME*, and *Vogue* magazines.

Myka resides in New York City with her husband and daughter. Find her websites beaumontetiquette.com (social etiquette) and beaumonttraininggroup.com (corporate training) and connect with her on Instagram, Twitter, or Facebook @mykameier.

Acknowledgments

To The Plaza Hotel and the amazing team there for being such phenomenal ongoing partners in running The Plaza Hotel Finishing Program, co-founded by Beaumont Etiquette and the hotel. In particular, I wish to thank Mr. George Cozonis, Ms. Ariana Swerdlin, and Ms. Abigail Hennelly.

Thank you to the amazing Beaumont Etiquette trainers and team members, whose passion and dedication to serving our clients internationally is so appreciated!

Index